Why Smart *M*en

Marry Smart *W*omen

Introduction

I'LL NEVER FORGET THE DAY I found the odd letter in my mailbox. It was addressed to me, in my own handwriting.

Dear Christine,
If all goes as planned you are 25 right now and in graduate school.

The note was a 1992 summer school assignment in which our class of 15-year-olds was instructed to write a letter to ourselves at age 25. A decade later, the program organizers made good on their promise to send on our predictions of life at age 25.

In addition to penning some humorous teen chatter *("I've met cool people and above all, guys: 4 guys liked me, 3 asked me out and 1 just had a crush on me"),* I had made a 10-year life plan.

- *Graduate from high school*
- *Go to a great college*
- *Go to law school*
- *Get married*
- *Raise kids*
- *Practice law*

I read and reread the letter, shocked, laughing, and crying all at once. It was as if the little girl in me was standing right there, asking for a progress report.

I did graduate from high school, and I went on to college. And I *was* in graduate school, although instead of studying law I was doing my doctorate in economic and social history. (I assumed the Christine of 15 would be OK with that.)

But I wasn't married (nor were there any immediate prospects in sight), and raising kids was the furthest thing from my mind.

It was the last line of the letter that most profoundly affected me.

Christine of 25, I hope things work out for you and you learn to find the balance between heart and mind.

Love, Christine of 15.

Why Smart Men Marry Smart Women is a book born out of research, survey data, and the personal experiences of thousands of young men and women nationwide, including my own. It's a book about shattering the bad news myths that smart, successful women can't have personal and professional happiness.

In 2006, high-achieving women are just as likely—if not more likely—to get married and have happy, healthy relationships as they pursue their career dreams.

Still, the bad news has a hold on the minds of so many accomplished young women—and their well-meaning relatives and advisors. When single, successful women in their late 20s and 30s meet for coffee, for drinks, at book clubs, and between classes to talk about love and relationships, they frequently ask themselves: Are men intimidated by smart women? Is he going to break up with me when he finds out I make more than he does? Are there men out there who are actually attracted to my intelligence and share my goals and ambitions for the future?

This new generation of high-achieving and single young women has a new set of challenges as they search for what I called at 15 the "balance between heart and mind." Our challenges are also our opportunities, and these new sets of choices build on the decisions of previous generations of smart, successful young adults.

In 1970, Elizabeth was a PhD candidate at Harvard's School of Public Health. A tall, slim, strawberry blonde, she was popular with the boys but hadn't met the right one yet. So she took out this ad in the *Harvard Crimson:*

> ### AFRAID OF PhDs IN MINISKIRTS?
>
> If so, ignore this! Two ravishing Harvard XXs desire to meet bright and interesting XYs (over 5'10", 21 yrs. plus) who are not threatened by intelligent attractive females. Box 1041.

Several men answered the ad, and she went out with one of them to a party, where she met Stephen, a law student at Harvard, who defied social conventions of the time: He was smitten with this perky, short-skirted PhD.

In 1971 they were married in a Catholic ceremony at St. Patrick's Cathedral. Instead of having children immediately, they pursued their careers. Sure, they intended to have a child eventually, but there was so much else to do. Beth founded a national public health organization and wrote several books. Steve made partner at his law firm. But the family pressure to have children was intense: A well-meaning aunt gave the pair a nightlight that blinked *Tonight's the night,* Beth's mother informed her that she couldn't resist a half-price sale on maternity clothes, and when Beth's first book was accepted for publication, her enthusiastic

"GUESS WHAT?" was met with an awkward silence when the news wasn't that grandchildren were on the way.

In 1975, Beth wrote *A Baby . . . Maybe: A Guide to Making the Most Fateful Decision of Your Life.* It was about how to make the choice to have a child—or not. It was a revolutionary book that documented the fears and hopes unique to her generation.

The book sold more than a million copies. The next year, Beth wrote a related book, *Boy or Girl?,* which examined the past and current state of knowledge about sexual selection. By December 1976, she was frequently on national television and radio shows discussing her findings—and her own indecision about having children. During one interview with the *A.M. Chicago* show, Beth was feeling queasy. She downed ginger ale and hoped she could get through the interview. Live on the air, the host asked Beth if she'd made up her mind about having children. Feeling a wave of nausea, she discussed the psychological quandary she and her husband were in. But she was pregnant, and the results of her decision were going to show soon.

I am the Baby . . . Maybe.

I was born in July 1977. My birth announcement includes the title of two of my mother's books: *A Baby . . . Maybe?* with a big YES! next to the title, and *Boy or Girl?* with "girl" circled. Mom and I appeared in *Newsweek* and *People* magazines: This pioneering woman had made her decision, and the whole country wanted a good look at me.

It's been 30 years since my mom published her provocative snapshot of the decisions facing her generation of successful women. Today, the question my generation faces is different. We can choose to have children or not; we can choose to marry or not. But for all those women who are smart, successful, and single in their 30s, there's a new question: Are today's high-achieving women overqualified for love?

Introduction

This book draws on six years of my academic research about changing dating and marriage trends in the United States.

For the first five years of my research, I was pretty depressed: The data from the 1970s, 1980s, and 1990s reported that successful women were less likely to marry. Those decades didn't seem like ancient history, so I applied the research to my life today. And as more and more women earned graduate degrees and higher salaries, I envisioned a generation of spinsters, overqualified for love.

I began this book when I was 27 years old, fresh from graduate school, and very much single. I'd ended two long-term relationships since college and had recently seen the *New York Times* wedding announcements for both of these men and their beautiful new wives. I'd just been dumped by a handsome businessman who told me that he couldn't date me because I was intellectually intimidating. On the face of it, it was kind of funny. I assume he meant it as a way to let me down easily, like saying "You're too good for me," when he really meant the reverse.

I immediately called my girlfriends to meet at a local bar. They ordered tequila shots to numb my pain and then proposed a champagne toast to my freedom from this idiot. I smiled and toasted with them. To hell with men, we declared. Back at home, I cried myself to sleep, terrified I'd be alone forever because no one wanted to date a dorky PhD.

Soon after, my mother started her questions. "So, did you meet anyone last night?" Each time I saw my grandmother, she would grab my left hand, asking, "Where's the ring? That PhD is fine and good, but you need your Mrs."

In early 2005, my research took a more positive turn: At first I uncovered one, and then another overlooked academic article suggesting that high-achieving women were marrying at increasingly high rates. These articles, mostly written by economists, explored what they called the "success penalty": Were women who had graduate degrees or a high income penalized in the marriage market? I discovered more academics interested in this topic at major research centers like Harvard, Princeton, and the University of Washington.

Using newly released government data, I ran my own analysis as well. I was shocked—and thrilled—to find out that the "success penalty" was a thing of the past. In the past 25 years—yes, since the not-too-long-ago 1980s—the tide has been turning slowly, and while most of us were still looking at old data and buying into the conventional wisdom, major demographic shifts were going unreported.

Nearly 3 million women in their 20s and 30s have advanced degrees, and 4 million women are already in the high-earning income brackets for their age groups.[1] Millions more women are on their way up, aspiring to ambitious careers, climbing the ranks of their companies, and working toward their graduate and professional degrees. The single women in this group want to know if their accomplishments are hurting their chances at personal happiness. Married women and those in long-term relationships wonder how they can balance their career with family.

Through the course of this book I've been inspired by the energetic, passionate, intelligent, and honest women who shared their experiences openly. Theirs are the voices of millions of successful young American women like you and me. C'mon girls, it's time for some good news.

Chapter 1

Meet the SWANS

IN HER 2005 BOOK, *Are Men Necessary?*, *New York Times* columnist Maureen Dowd lays out the conventional wisdom about successful women, dating, and marriage: "Men just want mommy," she writes. "Guys want to be in relationships with women they don't have to talk to." Thus, the book concludes, men fall in love with their assistants and housekeepers who will take care of them like their mothers did. The more successful a woman is, the less likely she is to get married.

Boiling down the headlines from the past several years, a casual reader would deduce that successful women are less likely to get married for a slew of seemingly logical reasons. One nationally publicized study found that men are intimidated by high-achieving women because men are fearful that these outgoing, ambitious women might leave them or cheat on them. The logic is that a woman who has her own money has more choices. And if she's not happy in her relationship, she can leave.[1]

A corollary of this argument is that relationships don't last when the woman makes *more* money than the man. Evolutionary biology dictates that men need to be the hunters: They need to be stronger, better, and more powerful than the woman to feel they have a place in the family. If a woman outearns her boyfriend or husband, she outmans him, and either he will feel so insecure that he withdraws from the relationship, or she will lose interest in such a girly man.

In addition, conventional wisdom subscribes to the notion that ambitious women aren't motherly or nurturing: Success is a masculine characteristic. How could a woman who aggressively negotiates multimillion-dollar contracts breast-feed and diaper an infant? And if a woman prioritizes her career, that means that she won't prioritize her man. At best, a high-achieving woman is depicted as an ice princess: beautiful, powerful, and untouchable.

For those successful women who are seeking a man, there's the assumption that they are interested in only a small, elite group of men. So no wonder they are single: They're fishing in a very small pond. For generations, women have attempted to "marry up" and have sought out men who are wealthier, more educated, taller, and more ambitious. Men, in turn, have had little problem "marrying down": seeking out wives who are less intelligent, petite, and financially dependent yet adoring. So what happens when more and more women themselves become wealthy, educated, tall, and ambitious? Is it lonely at the top?

Is today's successful, intelligent young woman overqualified for love?

In the words of President John F. Kennedy, "The greatest enemy of truth is not the lie—deliberate, contrived, and dishonest, but the myth—persistent, pervasive, and unrealistic."

This book shatters the myth that high-achieving women are at a disadvantage in the marriage market. New, large-scale survey data show that today's successful, well-educated young women will marry at the same rates as all other women—and that more income and education may in fact *increase* a woman's chances of marriage.[2]

Meet the SWANS: Strong Women Achievers, No Spouse

Swans are strong, graceful birds that sail alone for more than a third of their lives, but when they mate, as most do, they generally do so for life. The ancient Greeks believed swans were the birds of the Muses. In Norse mythology, the swan maiden was incredibly beautiful and desirable but impossible for a man to capture against her will. Hans Christian Andersen's ugly ducking struggled to find its place in the duck world until it realized its beauty as a graceful swan.

Revered for their composure and beauty, and sometimes feared for their strength, swans make a rather descriptive and colorful metaphoric parallel for the growing group of high-achieving single women in America today.

SWANS—Strong Women Achievers, No Spouse—are powerful, driven professionals who flock to urban areas and high-status jobs. Many have graduate degrees and earn high salaries: They are young lawyers making a mark, professors vying for tenure, journalists building relationships with high-powered sources, consultants advising senior executives, investment bankers embarking on a career in finance, and entrepreneurs starting a new business. SWANS are women of all ethnicities and religions, from all types of socioeconomic backgrounds, some with successful parents, many proud to be their family's first college graduates.

SWANS are a diverse group. There's the anesthesiologist who works out in a T-shirt that reads "Real Men Marry Doctors." There's the young executive who has founded a national organization to encourage female entrepreneurs. There are two black SWANS in Tucson who inspire their community, one through motivational speaking in her Baptist church, and another by her work as the local "Diva Dentist." But all these women have one thing in common: They wonder why, in spite of all their success, they are still single.

To be sure, there are some SWANS for whom the single life is something they do not care ever to change. Their image of the ideal, contented life has never included a husband; for these women, marriage or its absence is a nonissue. This book, however, is for the other SWANS, the ones who would like to marry someday, and for those who simply wonder, from time to time, why their love life seems to be taking a different path than they once imagined.

SWANS are smart women who want to know the facts behind the conventional wisdom of the day. With its blend of research, personal stories, and up-to-date national data, this book is written for intelligent, inquisitive young women who want answers.

The new and original information in this book is compiled from three sources: U.S. Census data, national opinion survey data that I commissioned for this book, and my personal interviews with more than 100 high-achieving men and women in nine cities nationwide.

The national government data comes from the 2005 Current Population Survey, a yearly nationally representative survey of 60,000 households conducted by the U.S. Census and Bureau of Labor Statistics. The opinion survey data was culled from my specially commissioned nationally representative Harris Interactive survey of 1,629 high-achieving men and women ages 25 to 40 conducted in January 2006 and a follow-up general omnibus survey of 2,073 men and women conducted in May 2006. Unless specifically cited, all opinion data presented in this book comes from my Harris Interactive research.

I conducted the interviews for this book from June 2005 through February 2006 in New York, Washington, Philadelphia,

Boston, Chicago, San Francisco, Los Angeles, Tucson, and Houston. Nearly all the interviews were conducted in person, in coffee shops, offices, restaurants, and private homes with high-achieving women *and* men, single, married, and divorced, in their 20s, 30s, and 40s.

Meet the SWANS: Strong Women Achievers, No Spouse.

Christina

Christina stared at the menu. California rolls, spicy tuna, salmon . . . she knew the drill. This was her fifth sushi date in two months. Since she had moved to New York City, men had been asking her out, and not just inviting her to dinner, but suggesting that they "go out for sushi." She didn't get it. Yes, sushi was trendy and could be expensive, but there were so many other nice restaurants in New York. Why were her dates specifying the food they were going to eat?

As her date pondered his dinner options—eel and cucumber or eel and avocado?—Christina wondered if she'd made the right choices herself. She was 29 years old and single. Somehow, it wasn't supposed to be this way.

Christina grew up in Charlotte, North Carolina. After college, she worked as a legislative assistant and public relations specialist in Washington, DC. Throughout her 20s, she dated her college boyfriend, but after five years the relationship fizzled. He had been "aggravating as all hell," Christina said, but he was a good person. "I liked being liked and being pursued by a guy. If he had proposed to me I would have accepted the ring." Still, when he moved away from Washington for a new job, she ended the relationship.

That's when the pressure began.

"When I was younger my mother said, 'Promise me you won't get married before you turn 25,' and then after I turned 25, I would hear, 'Well, I opened the life section of the newspaper and I didn't see your wedding announcement.'"

Christina followed a great job offer to New York, happy to experience "a new scene." This much sushi was certainly new, she said.

The next day at the office, she asked her boss what was up with all these guys. Why were they taking her out for sushi instead of Italian or French? "My boss laughed and said, 'Well, sushi is a dinner you don't linger over. You rarely get an appetizer, you order your sushi, you maybe order a beer to go with it or sake. You don't have coffee and you don't have dessert. When it's over, you know, if it's going well, he can say "Let's go out for a drink afterwards," or if it's not, you can call it a night.' And I realized it was brilliant. But I also realized I had a lot to learn about dating."

Christina, like many SWANS, wonders whether her decision to pursue her career is hurting her chances to find personal happiness with a man. SWANS worry that they might be intimidating. They wonder if men really want to share their lives with an equal or are looking for a docile subordinate—something these women are not.

And there are more SWANS than ever before.

Women are excelling in the academic world and becoming the strong achievers previous generations dreamed their daughters could be. In 1970, there were only 68 women enrolled in college per 100 men. In 2005, 133 women graduated from college for every 100 men, and women make up the majority, 57 percent, of college classes. This trend is expected to continue: In 2010, projections estimate there will be 142 college degrees awarded to women for every 100 that go to men.[3]

The gains for women in higher education are often even more impressive. More than three times as many women receive master's, doctoral, or professional degrees now than did in 1970.

The majority of all associate, bachelor, and master's degrees awarded during the 2000–2010 decade will be conferred on women, and by 2010 women will earn 151 master's degrees for every 100 awarded to men.[4]

In 1977, only 23 women received professional degrees, such as in law or medicine, for every 100 men. But today, about 50 percent of law school and medical school classes are women, and the vast majority of graduate students in the social sciences and health services fields are women. Even in the traditionally male fields of business and finance, women are excelling: Today more than 33 percent of MBA graduates are women. By 2010, women are expected to earn almost as many professional degrees as men. The projections suggest that women will earn 91 professional degrees for every 100 degrees conferred on men by 2010.[5]

This translates to major strides in the workplace. Women hold almost 50 percent of all corporate management positions, and an increasing number are attaining the top jobs and board seats.[6] Almost half of all privately held businesses are at least 50 percent owned by women.[7] And women hold twice as many senior management positions at large national companies as they did even in 1995.[8]

Women's strides in the workforce make staying single economically feasible. In addition, changing social mores and the widespread availability of birth control pills and other forms of contraception have lessened the pressure on Americans of all backgrounds to marry young.

The implications of these changes are felt nationally: In 1970, only 6 percent of American women between the ages of 30 and 34 had never married. Now it's 24 percent, four times greater. The median age of marriage for all women is about 25, but for women with a college degree it's closer to 27, and for those with a graduate degree it may be above 30 years old. For men, it's the same story:

Thirty-two percent of men age 30–34 have never married, more than quadrupling the 1970 rate.[9]

Today marriage is a choice, not an obligation. For a woman, a solid educational background and a good salary means she can be more selective: Instead of marrying a man for financial security or out of fear of being a spinster at 30, women may now choose to marry for compatibility, love, or companionship. For men, successful women represent an equal partner with whom to share life, not a constant drain on their hard-earned money.

Indeed, according to my new data, marriage is important for SWANS: 88 percent of single, high-achieving women reported that they would like to get married, and 86 percent of both high-achieving men and women said they wanted to get married. This is in keeping with the national data: The majority of men and women want to be married, and more than 90 percent of Americans do marry. In attitude surveys from the past several decades, three-quarters of men and women consistently report that a good marriage is "extremely important" to them—and an even higher percentage said they had positive feelings about being married.[10]

For most SWANS, there have been long-term relationships, dozens of men who were interested, and at least several conscious choices to remain single. In some cases, SWANS choose not to marry men who are alcoholics, verbally abusive, or completely stuck on themselves, even though these men had great money, power, and prestige. Why? Because as strong women who can achieve in their own right, they know they deserve more. Sometimes SWANS won't give a guy the time of day because he's too short, has a spare tire around his waistline, or talks too loudly. These may be petty reasons, but still, it's their choice.

SWANS are accomplished, smart young women who realize that the goal isn't to get married—it's to have a *good* marriage and to lead a happy and fulfilled life. Finding Mr. Right takes time and patience.

Antoinette

Antoinette stood at the podium, smiling as a room full of professional women clapped for her. She'd just delivered a speech about sisterhood and self-esteem as part of the empowerment workshops she runs through the YWCA.

Antoinette is an entrepreneur: She's a real estate agent who sold more than a million dollars' worth of properties in her first year in Tucson, a professional fund-raiser, and a motivational speaker. And though she'd had some dates here and there, at 36 she was getting frustrated.

As the youngest child of a Baptist minister father and a college professor mother, Antoinette has the gregarious nature of a preacher and the confidence of a woman who believes she can be a success in all aspects of her life. She grew up just outside of Chicago and moved out west in her late 20s.

She'd accomplished a lot—and she knew it. She had goals for her work, and she achieved them. But when it came to men, the same rules didn't apply.

Antoinette thought about her parents' marriage. Her mother had always earned more than her father, so Antoinette isn't one of those picky women who won't date a man because he doesn't have a certain job. Still, it is frustrating that she can't find a man who wants to be with her. "He should be proud and happy to have a woman like me that can take care of herself, and him, if necessary, and if you don't want that, I'm not the girl for you," she said.

Antoinette summed up her frustration: "I don't believe in 'You can't do it.' I want to date a man who is creative and likes to do a lot of different things. I don't need a man to fix me. But I need a man emotionally."

·   ·   ·

Articles, movies, and television reinforce the stereotype that successful women are cold, calculating, and, well, bitchy. According to my new survey data, high-achievers most commonly perceive entertainment media portrayals of successful women as aggressive and ambitious. "I would say the stereotype of a high-achieving woman is driven, smart, savvy, goal-oriented, and someone who is not going to let things get in her way. It's a cold stereotype," said Bill, a 32-year-old think tank researcher in Washington. Indeed, warmer characteristics such as kindness, creativity, and good parenting skills scratch the bottom of the list of qualities that pop to men's minds when they see successful women on TV.

Successful women suffer from a bad public image—and it's gone on for too long. A 1994 *Wall Street Journal* article coined the term "Hillary Wife," referring to the dual high-achiever couple of former president Bill Clinton and his also uber-successful wife, Hillary. The term frames the problems that ensue when a successful man marries a similarly successful woman, namely, how an accomplished wife "complicates" the male CEO's life as "schedules and interests collide."[11]

According to some media watchdogs, women are more vulnerable to bad reporting. "Women's lifestyle choices are subjected to greater scrutiny," said Julie Hollar, the communications director of Fairness and Accuracy in Reporting. "These articles are more about sparking debate and being controversial than about getting at some real truth."[12]

Still, these media caricatures reinforce the conventional wisdom that men are intimidated by successful, strong women. And SWANS are paying attention. Should women reinvent themselves to play down their *strong* side and play up the many other Ss of being a woman: *soft, sweet, sexy* women achievers? Evolutionary biology tells us that men are looking for youth and beauty in women: Make her pretty, docile, sweet, subordinate, and chaste, and she's the one. But these go-getter SWANS aren't docile or subordinate. Is it possible that both high-achieving men and women seek similar goals in life but are blinded by stereotypes?

Michele

Michele was perched on a stool at a bar in Denver, leaning back laughing. Her Seattle-based company had sent a select group of employees to Colorado for a one-month training session. While her coworkers were having beers and playing pool, Michele, 33, who was the designated driver for the evening, was having a debate with the bartender about the relative merits of professional hockey. The bartender's friend Dan walked in just as Michele was making an emphatic point about a recent hockey trade.

Dan was captivated immediately, and the two began chatting. Michele learned that Dan, 31, had grown up in Nebraska and had been hoping for a career as a professional baseball player but broke his back just after college. Currently he was working at the Enterprise Rent-a-Car at the local airport and owned his own record store. Tall and ruggedly handsome, Dan was "comfortable in his own skin," Michele said, and that, even more than his broad shoulders, was a refreshing change from the types of guys Michele had dated in the past.

Still, she wouldn't give Dan her number when he asked for it as the bar closed well after 3 a.m. The two agreed that they'd go skiing the next evening, and Michele took his number.

The next day she called and left a message for Dan when she knew he wouldn't be home. She canceled their skiing date but left the phone number at the hotel where she was staying. He called back almost immediately and they scheduled a date for the following evening. That night she called her girlfriend.

"I said, 'Uh-oh. I met this guy . . . and it isn't good,'" Michele recalled. Her friend knew what that meant and was sympathetic. The two women are devout Catholics, and Michele was sounding the alarm bell: She'd met a great guy, but he wasn't a practicing member of the church.

"My friend laughed. Even though I felt there was something different about Dan, some click, I had become friends with several men who weren't Catholic and who I wasn't going to have a relationship with. I could handle it, I said, and plus, it was only for a few weeks," Michele said.

Historic Shifts

SWANS worry that the conventional wisdom is true: that men are scared off, or turned off, by a woman's accomplishments. My new data show that nearly half of successful women believe their success is hurting their chances of getting married. Some 48 percent of single women ages 35 to 40 said they believed a woman who has achieved career or educational success would be *less* likely to get married, and 41 percent of all women with graduate degrees disagreed that men were more attracted to women who are successful in their careers.

"I'm sexy, attractive, entertaining, and I have wonderful friends and an interesting job. But I'm worried that by being interesting I might be scary and intimidating to men," said Emily, a 29-year-old credit card company consultant. "It seems like at least half of the men I meet are intimidated by me," says Adrianna, a dentist in Tucson. And Amanda, a petite 33-year-old museum curator, said there are days when she is terrified that she stayed in school too long and educated herself out of the marriage market.

Today's damaging myth represents the painful realities of recent generations: the grandmothers, and even the mothers, of today's young professional women. A woman who graduated from college in the 1920s had lifetime marriage probabilities that were fully 20 percentage points lower than those women of their generation who hadn't gone to college.[13] For women of the generation that has now risen to the highest ranks of most professions, women for whom graduate school became more common, higher education seemed to be the way to spinsterhood: In 1980, a woman with 19 years of education—that's college plus graduate school—had approximately a 66 percent chance of being married at age 40 to 44, compared to a woman with 12 years of education, who had an 83 percent likelihood of being married at that age.[14] Loosely translated, those statistics said, "Men don't make passes at girls who wear glasses." Sober statistics like these prompted *Newsweek* magazine in 1986 to famously declare that a single, college-educated 40-year-old woman had a better chance of being killed by a terrorist than of ever tying the knot.[15]

In the 1970s and 1980s, sociology embraced the findings of evolutionary biology as a way to explain the dating and marriage patterns of the time as somehow predetermined by nature. Academic articles routinely reported that women were more attracted to high-status men because such men were perceived as "providers," whereas men were attracted to pretty and docile women because they were perceived as "motherly" and fertile. Although feminism was making enormous legal strides, leading academic sociologists, buried in prehistoric eras, were oblivious to the major social changes going on all around them.

In real life, media reports and academic theories of the day notwithstanding, dating and marriage trends had already begun a historic shift. SWANS who are now approaching or in their 40s reflect happily on the differences between today and recent decades past. "It was very depressing in the 1980s to hear the stats," said Julia, a 37-year-old lawyer in New York who once considered herself, a successful married woman, to be "a fluke." Said Elaine, 43, "Femininity and power don't necessarily clash anymore. But when I was growing up, there was still a dichotomy."

Mothers of today's high-achieving young women marvel at the different paths their daughters are taking—and the myriad choices available to them.

Alice, 56, has her master's in public health and teaches at a prominent college. Yet she said she always felt that her husband had the "career" while she merely had a job. Her career, she said, was raising her two children.

Alice worked at prestigious posts at government agencies, helped launch grant programs for others studying public health, and worked full-time with the help of a nanny to watch the kids. "I was unusual then," she said. "I loved my work, but the family always came first—it had to."

Allison, 60, agreed that her experience in her 20s is very different from the options available to young women today. "I grew up, went to college, got married after my junior year, and finished senior year married," she said. "I followed my husband in his career and stayed home after my daughter's birth. At least until the children were in kindergarten, women stopped working when they had children. My mom had done that, and that's what I did, too." Allison's daughter is 28 and taking a completely different path: She has a graduate degree; she's seriously dating a smart, accomplished man; and she's looking forward to balancing children and a career simultaneously. "It's just a different world from what I was doing at her age."

Still, the negative conventional wisdom that successful women don't marry is routinely perpetuated in the media, by well-meaning but misguided relatives, and by young women themselves who are concerned that they have overqualified themselves for romantic happiness.

A 2005 letter to the Dear Abby advice column sums it up: A woman in her early 30s wrote to Abby after reading several articles "about how smart women are less likely to get married." She and her friends want to meet Mr. Wonderful and get married, she wrote, but she worries that "if we have to curtail our professional success, financial wherewithal and IQ to do it, how can a person even begin to do such a thing? . . . Help, Abby! What's the answer for smart, fun women who have their acts together? How can we best poise ourselves to find true love while being true to ourselves?" The young woman signed her letter "Losing Faith in Finding Mr. Right."

True to form, Abby had some good advice: "Stop reading defeatist newspaper and magazine articles. They'll only make you desperate, clingy and depressed—and none of those traits is attractive."[16]

For young women today, the "success penalty" has disappeared. According to my own analysis of up-to-date national data, education and income now have little negative effect on marriage rates, and in many situations, they actually act as benefits. Times have changed, but our perceptions haven't.

Chapter 2

Overqualified for Love?

IMAGINE, AS NEWSPAPERS and magazines recently have, the "plight of the high-status woman."[1] She is a well-educated young woman in her 30s, earns a good salary, and has a great social life—but she is single and is worried that her success might be the reason she has not met a man to marry. Any hint of bad news about the successful or talented has always made headlines, but media pessimism about the happiness and life balance of millions of young, career-oriented women has struck a chord nationwide.

The purported "news" was never good: Smart women are less likely to marry. Successful men are romantically interested only in their secretaries. And if a woman makes a lot of money, men will be intimidated. Conservative and liberal pundits alike mythologized the failure of feminism and the "waste" of these talented women who were searching for soul mates.

For a generation of SWANS—Strong Women Achievers, No Spouse—these myths have become conventional wisdom. If you attended a good school, have an impressive job, have career aspirations or dream of future success, men will find you less attractive. "I've been told by well-meaning relatives: 'Don't talk about work on a date, dumb it down, and it's bad to earn so much money because guys will be scared of you.' And I got the word 'intimidating' a lot," said Alexis, a 35-year-old lawyer in San Francisco.

She's not alone. Nearly half of single women believe their professional success is intimidating to the men they meet. Put another way, many high-achieving women think their success is not helping them find love. Some 66 percent of SWANS disagree with the statement "My career or educational success increases my chances of getting married."

Anne, a 30-year-old chief resident at a Boston hospital, said she doesn't think of herself as intimidating or uber-intelligent, but men seem to get that impression. "I was out with two friends from residency recently and I asked one of the married guys if he had any single friends to set me up with. He said, 'Oh, I get it, you're one of those super-smart superachievers that scare the men off.'"

"I didn't really know how to respond," Anne recalled of her colleague's character assessment, but other women have a strategy in place. They instinctually "dumb it down" or pretend to be someone they're not. When she was 35 and single, Julia, a lawyer in New York City, would play a game when she went to bars: "I told some guys I was an attorney and they ran away from me, and then other guys that I was a secretary at a law firm and at least for the short term they seemed more interested," she said. "There's the idea that high-achieving men don't like the competition, that they find us a little bit frightening, and get enough of that in the office. They want someone who is going to be at home."

This stunt became popular enough to inspire a *Sex and the City* episode. Miranda, the high-powered lawyer, tells a man she meets at a speed-dating event that she's a flight attendant. He tells her he's a doctor. Both of them are lying—she to diminish her status, and he to inflate it.

The stereotypes are powerful, and many high-achieving women

have created similar strategies. When Zara, a 26-year-old business school student, was an undergraduate at an East Coast Ivy League school, she and her friends used to fabricate identities that they assumed would be more attractive to men. "Senior year I spent spring break in Jamaica. My friends and I pretended we were from Southern Mississippi State University—which doesn't exist as far as I know—and put on southern accents to top it all off. We met all sorts of guys. We thought they'd be intimidated if they found out where we really went to school. They'd think we were argumentative, pushy, feminazis. Really, we're traditional in a lot of ways and are afraid of being judged negatively like that."

Given this prevalent conventional wisdom, it perhaps comes as no surprise that the romantic lives of accomplished women make front-page headlines only to tout bad news. "Men Prefer to Wed Secretary" announced UPI newswires in late 2004.[2] "Too Smart to Marry" read the headline in the *Atlantic Monthly* a few months later.[3] Newspapers throughout England, France, and Australia jumped on the bad news bandwagon in 2005: "Here Dumbs the Bride," "Keep Young and Stupidful If You Want to Be Loved," and "Alpha Females Use Their Heads, but Lose Their Hearts."[4]

Finally, these negative ideas hit a saturation point in 2005, when outspoken *New York Times* columnist and feminist Maureen Dowd embraced this well-worn myth. In a series of articles and columns in the *Times,* and then in a book, the Pulitzer prize–winning writer asked plaintively, "What's a Modern Girl to Do?"

Spreading Myths

Ironically, it's two successful women, a well-educated and influential economist in her 60s and a pioneering journalist in her 50s, both of whom accomplished so much ahead of their time, who have done the most to scare off younger ones from pursuing similar paths to success.

In 2002, Sylvia Ann Hewlett presented a study of high-achieving women who weren't marrying or having children at the same rates as other women. In her book *Creating a Life,* she stoked the flames of panic among successful women: "Nowadays, the rule of thumb seems to be that the more successful the woman, the less likely it is she will find a husband or bear a child." She argued that high-achieving women who were still single at age 30 had a less than 10 percent chance of ever marrying.[5]

Three years later, Maureen Dowd blamed her own single life on her career success. In her 2005 book *Are Men Necessary?,* Dowd told readers that she came from a family of Irish maids and housekeepers. Now in her 50s, she has achieved more than her great-aunts and grandmothers would have dreamed: She was one of the first women to have a regular opinion column in America's newspaper of record, she's written several best-selling books, and she has won the highest award in journalism. Writes Dowd, "I was always so proud of achieving more—succeeding in a high-powered career that would have been closed to my great-aunts. How odd, then, to find out now that being a maid would have enhanced my chances with men."[6]

These two books have had a profound effect on the way young, career-oriented women perceive their relationships.

Carolyn, 36, had recently ended a four-year relationship when the bad news books and articles began to garner large-scale media attention. She was getting anxious. "Should I be a little quieter? Should I listen more? Should I flatter more? Should I postpone talking about my stuff, should I put it off until he likes me for my personality? Should I laugh more? It feels fake, like a game, but I'm not sure what these studies are telling me to do."

Among single women in their 20s and 30s, the topics of marriage, career, and life balance are at center stage. Jill, Kim, Angela, and Star are members of a women's book club, and these bad news headlines were Topic #1 at a recent meeting. "I got that Maureen Dowd piece emailed to me by tons of people, including my mom, who wrote a header saying something like, 'According to this, you're never getting married.' Someone in the office emailed me as well. It was just amazing how one single article can have so much resonance," said Jill, 28, who works at a political nonprofit organization. "It was just depressing."

Kim chimed in: "I'm on the cusp of turning 30 and people are always complaining that smart women don't get married. You never hear about the relationships that are going well, the people who have found a great match. Instead, you hear about the single women who want to be married, as if that's the only story." Kim's own observations, however, are different: "It's a misconception that smart women don't get married. It's dated."

Star and Angela agreed that the media are on the wrong track: "The men I've dated *like* my career ambition," said Star. "They are looking for that. It's what they are most enamored with. And most of them have gotten graduate degrees themselves." But Angela, 31, added, "Getting those degrees delays the process. You tend to focus on school after a while. And that's when [women] freak out."

The deluge of dire findings about these women's chances at love don't help, either. In the years between Sylvia Ann Hewlett's research and Maureen Dowd's best-seller, two depressing studies garnered national attention.

In 2004, researchers at the University of Michigan published a study in the journal *Evolution and Human Behavior,* which, loosely summarized, found that the men in their sample would prefer to marry a woman whom they considered to be a subordinate, rather than a woman they considered to be a superior or a peer.

The media went into a feeding frenzy: "Powerful Male Looking for Maid to Marry,"[7] "Glass Ceilings at the Altar as Well as the Boardroom,"[8] "They're Too Smart for These Guys"[9] cried the news and editorial pages of major dailies nationwide. More than 100 newspaper and magazine articles, plus dozens of radio spots (aired multiple times each), plus TV commentaries—and, of course, countless Internet mentions—grew from the Michigan study.

Why question a real study, then, especially when many educated minds apparently had a chance to review it? Because the facts don't add up. This "news" was based on the opinions of 120 male undergraduates who were shown photos of a man and a woman, given a scenario about the person as either above or below them in an office hierarchy, and then asked a series of questions about that person.

So 120 guys just out of puberty said that they were more attracted to women who weren't that challenging to them. And this is national news?

To throw more fat into the fire, a multiuniversity English and Scottish study emerged a few weeks later, reporting that women with higher IQ scores were less likely to marry than women with lower IQ scores, whereas the opposite was true for men. This exhaustive study, well-researched and rigorous, followed nearly 900 men and women from age 11 through adulthood. With each up-tick in IQ scores, women were less likely to have married by midlife, but men were that much more likely to marry.[10]

Once again, the researchers were reputable. Plus, in this case, the number of individuals researched and the range in their backgrounds gave the study additional validity. Finally, the study's methods withstood examination of solid social science research procedure. With apparent justification, worldwide media gave the study thorough coverage. Scores of stories appeared on TV, radio, and in print—again, not to mention the volume on the Internet.

Why, then, cast any doubt on the results, or on the media's exhaustive international coverage of the announcement?

Here's why: This study was conducted on men and women born in *1921*—men and women who would be 85 years old today. These women were born seven years before the UK granted equal voting rights to women. When these seniors were coming of age in the early 1940s, women had to resign their jobs upon marriage and top universities were still closed to female students. Not until these women reached their 50s would equal pay be implemented in the Civil Service. The results may be valid, but the idea that the gender norms of Grandma's generation are newsworthy and applicable to the lives of young, smart women today is laughable.

Does Bad News Sell?

Clearly, these studies didn't merit the vast attention they received. So why do the news media and popular culture outlets so eagerly perpetuate destructive bad news for successful women? Harvard professor Russell Muirhead has suggested that the average Jane and Joe are comforted to think that unusually smart, successful people are living less happy lives, "that for all educated women know, they might not know enough to find love."[11]

A magazine journalist, Eileen, age 34, said she understands the media craze for bad news. "There's a very powerful need to create a subcategory of people to feel superior to, so if you've chosen to give up your career to get married and have kids, you might feel like it's only fair that successful women shouldn't get married. You made your choice and they made theirs," she states bluntly.

But then Eileen pauses, and considers yet another option: that the quest for Mr. Right is long and full of tough moments along the way, and doom-and-gloom articles will always reflect the depression of young women after *yet another* bad blind date, another failed relationship, another guy who didn't call.

"The whole dating thing just feels hard, and sometimes we just want data that support the way we feel. Even if the news is great in the long run, it's still hard, and we like to wallow a bit," Eileen said.

Another reason these dire statistics have such resonance: They were true for our aunts and mothers and older mentors. In 1980, the median age of marriage nationwide for women was 22. But according to the 1980 Census, a woman with a graduate degree was twice as likely to still be single between the ages of 25 and 34 than a woman who had a college degree or less. In fact, 1 in 5 women with graduate degrees (20.5 percent) had not married by age 34, compared to 1 in 10 women without graduate degrees (9.6 percent).[12]

So when newspapers report that women achievers find it difficult to find men, it resonates with a lot of ambitious SWANS who aren't getting what they want quite yet. And though we all need a good bitch session every now and then—and though it always seems worse for *us* than for anyone else—the news, girls, is good.

High-achieving women marry at the same rate as all other women; they just do so a bit later in life. Smart women *do* get married. Men *do* make passes at girls who wear glasses. And though some men are looking for women to play fetch for them, there's certainly no shortage of men who would much prefer to volley with an equal.

The Real Story

To get numbers to tell a story, it's necessary to pull out some particular groups to test. Most researchers use education and income as a substitute for achievement, which, let's face it, is hard to define and measure precisely, even if we all agree we know what it means. Others look at the sexiness of status (Is having a high-powered job related to sexual attraction?). And still others explore power and ambition.

The original research presented in this book defines high-achieving women as women with a graduate degree—a master's, doctoral, or professional degree in any field—and/or an income in the top 10 percent of women in their age group; that means women ages 24 to 34 who, in 2005, earned $50,000 per year or more, and women ages 35–40 who earned $60,000 per year or more.

Certainly there are many SWANS who don't fit this rigid national numerical definition. There are towns and cities where earning much less than $50,000 earns a woman a place in the top 10 percent of earners in her area. There are plenty of successful, talented, and ambitious women who have chosen not to go to grad school or who have taken prestigious but lower-paying jobs in public service, the arts, politics, or diplomacy. They are women who aspire to be out-standing at whatever profession or activity they choose. Success, and the aspiration to succeed, comes in many forms. Better still, success is sexy, and the new numbers show that higher income and educa-tion increases a woman's chances of marriage.

Sex and power are often linked, but most sociological theories (and media headlines) predict that it is women who will flock to high-powered men and find them the most attractive, whereas men will be drawn to docile and subordinate women. Yet a 2005 article in the *American Journal of Sociology,* overlooked by the media, reports just the opposite: High-status and powerful *women* are rated as more attractive. Based on a study of interpersonal relationships in 60 different communities nationwide, the author concludes that women in positions of power are sexier to men than are more sub-ordinate women.[13]

Research by Megan Sweeney, an assistant professor of sociology at the University of California, Los Angeles, adds another data point to the good news plot: Higher-earning women marry at higher rates. Among white women, a $10,000-per-year increase in salary can mean a 7 percent increase in the likelihood that she will marry within a year. For black women, that same salary bump increases the likelihood of marriage by more than 8 percent.[14]

And the trend only improves. Economist Elaina Rose at the University of Washington studies the relationship between marriage rates and education level, and how the two have affected each other over time. By looking at U.S. Census records going back several decades, Rose has tracked the diminishing marriage "success penalty." Twenty-five years ago, a woman with a graduate degree was 13.5 percent less likely to have ever married at age 40 to 44 than a woman with only a high school diploma. In percentage terms that's a big number. By the 2000 Census, that penalty had largely disappeared.[15]

There's already plenty of data to anticipate more good news in the upcoming 2010 Census. The Current Population Survey (CPS), a yearly representative sample of 60,000 households nationwide, tracks education, income, and marriage data. Based on 2000 and 2001 CPS data, Heather Boushey at the Center for Economic Policy Research in Washington, DC, demonstrated that working women between the ages of 28 and 35 who earn more than $55,000 per year (well above the U.S. median) or have a graduate degree are just as likely to be married as other women who work full-time.[16] According to the newest available data, the 2005 CPS, for women with an advanced degree and for women who earn in the top 10 percent of all female earners for their age group, there's no marriage penalty. High-achieving women marry at the same rates as all other women; they just do it a little later.

It's common for high-achieving women to marry for the first time at age 30, according to CPS data. So in that first wave of late-20s weddings, successful women may be feeling a little panicky.

Some 55 percent of women with graduate degrees have married by age 29, compared to 61 percent of other women.

But then the tide turns: It's significantly more likely that a woman with a graduate degree will walk down the aisle in her 30s than a woman with a college degree or less. And SWANS' own experiences reflect this.

Jessica, a 35-year-old entrepreneur, has an explanation for the difference in timing: "The more successful woman, or the higher IQ woman, might be less likely to get married young because she has the intellect to see through the garbage that some other people might not care to see through. She has the awareness, and has been raised to ask the questions that will immediately be obstacles to getting married." Jessica has many smart friends who found their match and married in their 20s, but she is proud of her decision to continue to search for the right man for her, instead of settling. For women in their 30s, she added, "I would say that our education is helping us—we now have the balance, the yin and the yang, the softness and business success."

Kama, a consultant in Chicago, said she and her friends, all in their early 30s, have been doing some studies of their own to test whether their degrees are holding them back on the dating scene—and the results have been promising. "I had a friend who did speed dating with 28 guys. In half of those quick introductions she said she went to Harvard Business School and in half she didn't mention it. She got the same number of ask-outs from each pool. It's a small sample, but I hope that's a good sign."

For Julia, the New York lawyer who told men at bars that she was a secretary, things changed at 36. "Yeah, then I met Adam," she said with a shy smile, unconsciously playing with her wedding ring. The couple met at a friend's party, and Julia, who had all but given up on meeting someone special, said she could tell from the beginning he was different. So she told him she was a lawyer.

"Adam finds my intelligence more of a turn-on. He can talk to me and I understand him. From the time we met, it was like a first date that never ended. We were engaged in four months and married in under a year. For the first time, I felt I didn't have to hide parts of myself."

Melissa and Kristen, both in their late 20s, don't understand why any woman would be concerned. They are both seriously dating men who value their intelligence, and they feel confident that their good experiences are the norm. "These studies are complete crap. Danny doesn't know anything about finance," said Kristen, who is starting a new job as an investment banker at a leading firm. "He runs a wine import business. I can think of so many examples where guys are sometimes attracted to beautiful, blond, popular girls when they are young, but when they are older, they are looking for girls who are brighter, and have more intellectual qualities."

"Most of my guy friends would say they have to be able to have a conversation with their wives," said Melissa, who has just finished her master's degree. "I think most of my [male] friends went to good schools and are surrounded by smart women. My brother has a JD/MBA and he's married to a woman who is a doctor, and they got married later. More so now than 50 years ago, men want women who are their equals or superiors."

Melissa's boyfriend, Michael, is proud of her successes. "When I meet one of Michael's friends, they'll say, 'I heard that you dogged him on the ski slopes and you're smarter than he is,' and you know, men want that, a girl who will challenge them and not say 'Yes, dear, here's your scotch and soda.' I mean, he was the one who told his friends that to begin with."

"What I think they are mixing up in those studies is that men do like to be taken care of, but taking care of a guy doesn't mean that you are subordinate. I would make a drink, but then I'd sit down and talk to him about any given issue," concluded Kristen.

Like more and more SWANS, these women's instincts are borne out by the current numbers. For instance, according to data from the 2005 Current Population Survey, an unmarried 30-year-old woman is more likely to have made it to the altar by age 40 if she has a graduate degree than if she doesn't. There's a two-thirds chance that a 30-year-old woman will marry if she has a college degree or less, but there's a three-quarters chance she'll be a bride if she has an advanced degree. By ages 35 to 39, a higher percentage of high-achieving women have walked down the aisle than their less accomplished sisters.

Geography doesn't matter either: In cities and suburbs, large cities and small cities, these data hold true. In Chicago, Dallas, Houston, Los Angeles, New York, Philadelphia, Phoenix, San Antonio, and San Diego—the largest U.S. population centers where SWANS flock—high-achieving women marry at the same rate as all other women in their area.

The Price of the Success Myth

New data reveal that a high-achieving woman is more likely to marry just the kind of man conventional wisdom would suggest would be intimidated by her apparent success. More than half of married women with graduate degrees are married to men *without* graduate degrees. Clearly, men who aren't intimidated by SWANS do exist.

Having a higher income than one's significant other doesn't make much of a difference in women's marriage rates. So the idea that men are intimidated by a woman who might outearn them doesn't hold true, either. Yet the myth that successful women are overqualified for love seems to persist.

This myth has high costs for today's SWANS. It's a self-fulfilling prophecy that, although it doesn't affect SWANS' marriage rates, does cause pain and anxiety and may lead to some undesirable choices. Women who are panicked about their marriage prospects are more likely to give off negative or desperate vibes to men, and SWANS who believe that men will be intimidated by their education or success may find that it's really ego and attitude—not their success—that are getting in the way. For other women, the relentless pressure from relatives and bad news in the headlines makes them insecure enough to stay in bad relationships too long.

"I was ready to break up with [my ex-boyfriend] about four years ago—and I stayed two years too long—and part of the reason I stayed was what so many women are thinking: Do I want to go through it all again? Do I really want to date again? The whole mess of it, the uncertainty of it," said Carolyn, 36. "So you rationalize in your mind that you can stay, that you should keep doing this because it's your only shot."

Carolyn blames herself for the failure of the relationship. In the past few years, she founded her own advertising company and devoted a lot of time to building her client base. "Creating my business was my priority, so it probably overwhelmed my personal life," she said. Based on the many articles she has read about successful women destroying their relationships, men can't handle smart women. So part of her believes that her relationship failed because it was her fault: She is too bright.

Even though the aggregate data show that success doesn't hurt SWANS in the dating game, the suggestion alone makes many of these women angry. "Even if it's just the perception, it puts no pressure on men and lots of pressure on women. That pisses me off. It's unfair," said Laura, a strikingly beautiful lobbyist in Washington, DC. "The pressure makes otherwise totally cool women seem anxious, desperate, and 'crazy' to find a man. These women aren't crazy, but they are in their early to mid-30s and haven't found someone, and because they want kids, they do things perceived as desperate." Laura ended a one-year relationship a few months earlier and said she hasn't given herself time to heal because all this panic in the air is making her nervous. "I have to get back in the zone and date guys before it's too late."

John, 29, a professor at a prominent business school, noted that this effect is obvious on the male side of the market as well. "In recent years it feels like the balance of power in dating has totally shifted. It used to be women who were totally in control. Now it seems like the men hold all the cards. Women just seem really anxious to partner up and seem to put up with an astonishing amount of messing about from men. It's got to the point where I have started to look for the rare women who simply won't put up with my crap," he said.

But SWANS should relax and be themselves: Again, there is good news in newly released 2005 Current Population Survey data. Successful women in their 30s have options—and SWANS in their late 30s are significantly more likely to walk down the aisle than their less accomplished sisters. For 35-year-old women with graduate degrees, their chances of marrying by age 40 are 25 percent higher than for their sisters without the advanced degrees. Less educated women marry earlier; those brides gliding down the aisle in their 30s are more likely to be SWANS.

SWANS Have More Fun

SWANS are leading ever-richer lives. Young women are pursuing education and dream careers and embarking on international adventures of their own. "Women who are successful aren't trying to just get married. They want to travel, be cultured. If we're single, it has a lot to do with our decisions," said Kim. Her book club partner

Jill agreed: "We're not in a rush. A lot of women are going to graduate school, and it strains the relationship. My mom followed my dad everywhere. It's not for lack of opportunity that I'm single; it's because of a generational change of priorities. If you are successful, there's no big rush to have anyone take care of you."

There's some encouraging news that this strategy works. Up to a certain point, waiting a bit longer to get married, and pursuing higher education and career interests along the way, may increase the chances of marital bliss. Women without a college degree are almost twice as likely to divorce as their better-educated sisters. It's certainly true that more educated and successful women are less likely to remain in abusive marriages, and couples with more intellectual and monetary resources are more likely to seek marriage counseling when their relationship is in trouble.[17]

"In my 20s, I focused [on] and prioritized my professional life and I didn't do the same thing with my personal life," said Patricia, a 32-year-old Washington attorney. "There are more opportunities for women, and we have the ability to make the same choices as men—so women aren't settling for a relationship they don't want or need. If it's just about want, it's a more difficult thing to achieve. When women needed a provider, the arrangement was clearer. Now it just takes a bit longer to find the right guy."

Chapter 3

Hi, I'm Fabulous

MUSIC POUNDING IN HER HEAD, Christina did a quick check of her makeup in the ladies' room and then made her way to the back corner of the bar. Three dark leather couches hugged a low wood table—a table that, as per usual, had a small "Reserved" sign on it, two bottles of expensive vodka, and an assortment of mixers, ice, and glasses. Three well-dressed, slightly balding men sat comfortably, each marking one couch as his territory, arms resting on the back of the soft leather, legs spread out, filling the space. Perched on the arms of the couches or standing, hips cocked to one side, cocktails in hand, were eight women. These were Christina's girls, and apparently, these were the men they'd glommed on to for a night of free drinks and fun.

Christina, a North Carolina native, moved from Washington to New York at 29 years old, after her five-year relationship ended. With a great new job and a set of single, attractive girlfriends, Christina was living the "club scene" to the hilt. She was getting used to this "other echelon of investment banking types where you'd go to clubs and people would have their tables . . . and champagne and there would be no check."

But it made her uncomfortable to watch her friends flock to

these men. It was too loud in these bars to have a conversation, so all you knew was that the guy had enough money to buy expensive liquor, she said.

"I mean, I had never experienced this kind of feeding frenzy on any rich dude who happened to be in the picture. 'Hook up with some guy who will pick up our tab' was the name of the game. So many of these men acted like they had hit the candy store jackpot. And the women were going for it." For Christina, who was just interested in going out and having fun, female friends, it was an adventure. Her closest confidants weren't in New York City, and most were in relationships, so the "club girls" provided entertainment. And free drinks from the men.

Just two weeks before, Christina had been dumped by an investment banker, the kind of guy who might have bought a bottle of vodka for all of them tonight had he still been in the picture. She was 30, and "I'd always figured by 30, you know, I'd be on my way to getting married." He was a nice guy, but one "who really just wanted to party and play and not be tied down," she said. They had been together only a few months, but she was stinging from the rejection.

"You know, he just can't handle being with you because you're too much for him," one of her girlfriends said right after the breakup. "You're a challenge because you're a smart person and . . . he wasn't ready for a commitment with someone like you." Those words seemed to drown out the loud techno music in the club as she approached her group of friends for another night out.

In addition to all the usual dating fears and questions, SWANS like Christina wonder if it is their career or educational success that's holding them back. How should they talk about their job when they first meet a man? Should SWANS downplay their accomplishments so they don't look boastful? And do men really break up with SWANS because they are too smart and "challenging," as Christina's friend wanted her to believe?

Or might a woman's intelligence and accomplishments, combined with all her other good qualities, actually be a "bonus" in the eyes of men?

Relationship advice writers think so. Writes one in a blast email to thousands of female subscribers: "Success won't buy you love, affection or get you shortcuts to a great situation with a man . . . but it just might help get you in the door."[1]

The Dating Game

Searching for a perfect match is hard. It's the search for that perfect blend of attraction, common values, and compatibility. According to a 2006 Pew Internet & American Life Project survey, 55 percent of singles actively seeking dates said it was "difficult to meet people." In fact, the survey found that of seeking singles, 36 percent had not been on any dates in the past three months.[2]

Among high-achieving men and women in the Harris Interactive study commissioned for this book, an even greater percentage of singles complained about the difficulties of dating. Seventy-six percent of single women and 74 percent of single men said they found it hard to meet people they would be interested in dating or having a relationship with—and setups are few and far between. Only one-third of SWANS said that their friends often introduce them to prospective dates.

But it's not that singles are too busy; the majority of high-achieving single women said they had enough time for their personal lives. Instead, many SWANS who are building their careers say their real worry is that their ambitions and previous successes are making them less attractive to men.

Raquel, a 25-year-old investment banker, said men she met at bars would "literally walk away" when she told them the name of the prestigious bank where she works, so she stopped telling men what she did for a living. "Then I met this one guy who was all proud of himself and said he was an investment banker. I was excited—so I decided to tell him I was, too. But his game was ruined when I told him where I worked. He was at a much smaller place, and he didn't know what to do. He stuck around and kept talking to me, but he called me 'Cutie' all night after that." Guys, she said, are thrown off guard by successful women. "Especially the guys that are relying on their credentials to attract women. But then you start wondering if a club is the right place to meet someone anyway."

Indeed, Raquel may have diagnosed her own problem: Few Americans meet their spouse or partner in a club. According to the Pew Internet and American Life Project, only 13 percent of couples who are married or in a serious long-term relationship met at a bar, nightclub, café, or other social gathering. The most common places to meet a match were work or school groups and introductions through family and friends.[3]

Whether SWANS are talking to men in clubs or friends' cocktail parties, high-achieving young women are conscious about how they talk about their accomplishments.

How to Talk About Success

Because two-thirds of SWANS do not think that their professional success increases their chances of getting married, they have come up with some tricks to avoid potentially uncomfortable subjects.

Many SWANS report that avoiding the "what do you do" conversation has become second nature. "I usually play down my career," said Anne, a 30-year-old medical resident at a Boston hospital. "I say I work in an ER but I don't say I'm a physician if they ask. I'm not coy, but I do play it down because there's always some reaction that I don't enjoy."

Jody, a 31-year-old postdoc in brain development, agreed: "When I'm on a date, I try not to talk about my work," she said. "Instead, I play up other aspects of myself: politics, style, and design. I can be funny, and I think I have a lot of fun conversations. All that is more important."

Talking about music, sports, or just about anything other than a 30-second résumé synopsis is a great way to spin success, counsel relationship coaches. Making a joke about herself or not telling a man what she does is a way to "keep him guessing" and avoid the "predictable, emotionally unengaging, and rational conversation about your real jobs."[4]

Adrianna, a black dentist in Tucson, said she "eases men in" to her self-made success. She put herself through dental school and owns her own practice, not to mention a house in a nice neighborhood and a car. But Adrianna, 42, will tell a man she first meets that she's in the "dental field." The conversation usually goes like this: "They ask, 'You're an assistant? A hygienist?' They never think I'm a dentist. They are floored when I say that I've been a dentist for 15 years, and that I own my own practice. I'll try to deflect and ask them what they do, but when it comes back to me, the most shock comes when they ask who I work for. I work for myself. They think I'm kidding."

To avoid awkward interactions, Adrianna now focuses the conversation on the guy for as long as possible. "The idea is to not show them everything up front. Let them get to know you. And then, when I do invite them in, I blow them away."

Alexis, a 35-year-old lawyer in San Francisco, said postponing the career conversation was a lesson she learned early on. When she lived in Arizona, she started deflecting questions about what she did because she wanted to avoid the lawyer jokes and questions seeking advice about "their friend who got arrested for DWI."

When Alexis joined a friend of a friend for a Fourth of July escape in Lake Tahoe, there were eight people sharing a small house, most of whom had never met before. On the first night, one woman suggested that instead of introducing themselves to each other in the usual way—by asking what each did as a career—the group should try to get to know each other by learning about each person's interests and passions. "We had a great time. At the end of the weekend we guessed before we told each other what we did for work," Alexis said. "It was great for me because I don't identify primarily with my job. But there were people who were visibly uncomfortable not talking about their job."

Indeed, my new research finds that 32 percent of single high-achieving women tend to minimize their career or educational success in conversation when they first meet someone they might be interested in dating. High-achieving men say they do the same thing.

"High-achieving women shouldn't shove success down the guy's throat," said Allegra, a married 35-year-old entrepreneur in Los Angeles. "You don't need to prove anything. Your accomplishments come out. It naturally follows in your conversation—and they can see it," she said. "Instead, on a date, ask them about themselves and be genuinely interested. Let them ask you questions about yourself. Otherwise you are trying to prove to them that you are legitimate. It's much more interesting to come across that sort of information than to perceive that someone is giving you a résumé lecture. People who brag about their careers, it's like the cowboys with the big hats, no cattle. If you show off, you've got nothing."

But downplaying and hiding accomplishments gets frustrating, said several SWANS. Zara, a business school student, said she used to hide her educational background; now she uses it as a filter. "If someone is intimidated, I don't want to talk to them anyway," she said. Melissa, 27, agrees: "I tell anyone who asks what I do. It's clearly something I'm proud of because I put my mind to it." Melissa earned her master's in international relations and now works at a top investment bank. "It's never something I would hide. If they didn't like it or were intimidated, they weren't the guy for me."

Melanie, a first-year business school student from California, said she is hesitant to tell people she is getting her MBA because of the stereotypes that go along with the degree. "MBAs are supposed to be heartless, profit-driven, sell-outs, and cocky. It's something I think about as a woman," she said. "But I've stopped apologizing and explaining myself. There are things that I've done that are hard to be humble about. I made a movie at 23. I'm careful not to bring that up on the first date. It has to come up pretty soon, though, since you tell stories about yourself and hopefully in a funny, modest way."

Nadia and Shayna, two medical residents, have had similar experiences and worry about the assumptions that men make about their personalities based on their professional choices. "When I tell guys that I'm a doctor, it's very unexpected," Nadia said. "A guy in a bar comes up to me, I'll tell him I'm a health professional," Shayna agreed. "And they always assume I'm a nurse. But it's so smooth when I tell guys that I'm a nurse. They smile and that's the end of it." Nadia chimed in, frustrated: "And when I tell them I'm doing anesthesiology, they say, 'Why aren't you in pediatrics? Don't you like kids?'"

At a recent book club meeting, Kim, a 29-year-old attorney, and Jill, a 28-year-old nonprofit manager, also worried that their choice of careers sent an immediate message about their personality that wasn't quite what they wanted to represent. "I won't say I'm a lawyer. It's not something I volunteer. I feel like some men immediately type me," said Kim. "I don't think it's true that men are threatened or intimidated, but they do stereotype you. Still, I hate games, and really, what's the point of hiding what you do?"

Other women are aggravated that they are even *considering* such nuances about their chosen careers and considerable accomplishments. "What you do is what you do," said Rebecca, a 32-year-old marketing executive. "You work so hard to get to the place that you are, so why wouldn't you want to share that with somebody who may actually become a part of your existence? If you say matter-of-factly, 'This is what I do for a living, I'm happy, I've got a really good life, thank you very much,' it doesn't seem to me to be in and of itself particularly confrontational in any way."

Still, the stereotypical successful woman is ambitious, cold, and calculating—just the opposite of a warm, motherly figure—and many SWANS feel they are constantly fighting against this stereotype in their dating lives. Cynthia, 34, described it as a "tap dance" where a woman attempts to show her strength and softness at the same time. "We've become quite proficient at that dance—if that's a priority for us," she added.

There is some finesse involved. "You don't want to preempt those concerns by announcing that you'd be a good mom on the first date. It's like saying, 'Really, date me, please!'" said Raquel, 25, but she said she does try to communicate that there is more to her than her demanding business career.

"I think a lot of men are concerned that I won't make him my first priority. But what a lot of men don't realize is that just because we are smart and successful, doesn't mean we won't prioritize our relationships or our families," said Kama, a 28-year-old Indian-American management consultant. "I'll move for his career—and I hope he might move for mine, too."

Antoinette

"I left 'chocolate cities' on the East Coast, full of black men, after I got my graduate degree," sighed Antoinette, a full-bodied black woman with sparkling eyes and a contagious laugh. "And right out of grad school I realized I was supposed to get married. My mom's friends would ask her about me and it's hard for her to say I'm not married."

A single black woman in Tucson has to make an effort if she wants to meet men, Antoinette decided. And though she had been in no rush to settle down, she was in her late 30s, and it was time to work on it.

She thought about her ideal man: It was a long list, and Antoinette realized that she could be missing a blessing. "I was creating a perfect human being—that's not reality, and I'm not perfect either. It'd be exhausting to date the perfect man because then I'd have to be perfect." She settled on a few key qualities: He needs to be kind and have a sense of spirituality and faith, ambition, and creativity. "And what if he's a landscaper and I'm a big executive and I say I can't date him? No. This might be the man that rubs my feet with his rough hands. I couldn't overlook that. But I don't care if a guy makes less than me—he's still paying for dinner," she laughs. "I mean it!"

One of her friends had joined a dating service where, for a set fee, the company would match her with 10 men. Antoinette's friend fell in love with man #3, and after they were married she offered to transfer the remainder of the membership to Antoinette, who had been on dating hiatus for more than a year.

But her experiences with the dating service weren't promising. At times, Antoinette said, the men were downright terrible. "I said 'Lord, what am I doing wrong?' And then I said, well, let me just focus on my work. It's not working out over here, so I'm going to focus over here. I'm going to take time off from dating."

She bought a four-bedroom house for herself and spent several months getting it ready. One evening, she was telling two male friends about her fantastic new place—and she was surprised when they cautioned her not to tell too many people about it. "They said men would be intimidated by that, and that I should have waited until I got married to buy a house. I thought, well, that's stupid. Another friend took me to Home Depot and helped me buy tools. That's what a man should do," she said firmly.

With most men, she downplayed her success: "I'd never mention I had a master's and never talked about money. They would leave the table and not know a lot about me." She wouldn't invite a man over to her home, and she was careful about talking too much about her speaking engagements or other activities that drew attention to her entrepreneurial bent. She decided that in the future, that was going to change. "Now I talk. I say, this is who I am. I tell them what I do and what I like. I don't like camping. I'm not that girl. My idea of camping is a hotel without a lobby. And that's important for them to know. It's about emotional honesty," she said.

The Price of Love

Some women speak about their dating life in business terms: bottom lines and corporate personality tests. One SWANS said her family asks "What's new" in her dating life "once a quarter," and likens the update to an "earnings report." Another talks about getting the "comps" on various men she meets. A SWANS in California talks about her dating BATNA, using the acronym for a negotiation strategy where one side decides its sticking point, or its best alternative, to a negotiated agreement. When her dating

BATNA is high, she is more discerning about the men she dates and feels she has the power. More than a few women will describe their ideal man in terms of scores on a Myers-Briggs personality test. One is looking for an ENTJ (an extroverted person who also scores high on the intuition, thinking, and judging scales), another for a sensitive type, and a third said she's an I (an introvert) and needs a similar type of man. "And if he's an S-type, a data-driven guy, it's a deal breaker," said another.

"The way women talk about relationships—in demanding tones, talking about having structure—it's interesting and slightly bizarre," said Laura, 29, who works at a Washington, DC, think tank. "It's like you're about to put out an annual report on past performance and future projections."

Yet this kind of language is increasingly common. In 2004, Rachel Greenwald's best-seller *Find a Husband After 35 (Using What I Learned at Harvard Business School)* captured this new lingo. In a businesslike tone that could terrify softer single souls, she writes about the marketing, packaging, branding, and advertising women over 35 must do to find a man. "It costs money to find a husband," she states bluntly. There are direct costs—the costs of dating service memberships, parties, and nights out—and there are indirect costs of new clothing, push-up bras, and makeup. Greenwald recommends that a single woman spend 10 to 20 percent of her annual income on her quest and put this money into a separate bank account labeled "The Husband Search." She advises women who are worried about finances to borrow from friends or dip into savings.[5]

With this kind of advice, it's no wonder the for-profit matchmaking and dating industry is booming. According to one estimate, it's a $1 billion business in the United States, with more than 850 online dating services representing nearly 50 percent of the market's value.[6]

Money has always been central to the modern dating game, but during most of the second half of the 20th century, it was the man who would pay for dates or treat a woman to dinner and dancing, and a woman's direct costs would be minimal.[7] With the advent of online dating, matchmakers, and dating coaches, the tide has turned. Increasingly, single women are taking on larger costs in courtship rituals.

SWANS have resources—and they have no qualms about spending money on their dating life. To post and exchange emails with potential dates using online sites like Match.com or eHarmony can range from $12 to $50 per month. A night of speed dating can cost between $50 and $150, factoring in the price of admission and drinks for the evening. In major cities, dating coaches charge upwards of $150 per hour, and matchmakers can cost up to $15,000 for elite services.

In the past decade, online dating has gone mainstream. Posting a profile online is no longer seen as a sign of desperation; in fact, it's practically considered a rite of passage for young singles. According to a 2006 Pew Internet & American Life Project survey, 37 percent of single Internet users who are actively looking for dating partners have gone to online dating web sites. Of these, 17 percent report that they have started a long-term relationship or married someone they met on one of these sites.[8]

Among high-achievers, online dating is even more commonplace. My survey data show that 48 percent of single high-achieving women and 55 percent of single high-achieving men have used an online dating service. "Online dating is the most effective and efficient way to exponentially increase your possibilities. And the idea that it's efficient appeals to high-achieving women," said Kristin Kelly, a spokesperson at Match.com. SWANS are more likely to be proactive about dating, said Kelly, because they are goal-oriented and clear about what they want in many other aspects of their lives. "It's a level of self-confidence, of describing yourself and putting yourself out there. And that's what high-achievers do. When women make the first move they are more likely to get a response than when men initiate," Kelly said.

"We met on Match.com," said Jackie, 30, describing how she met her husband. "I realized that I had to stop meeting people at bars and clubs, and joined, and he emailed me. I was about to get off the service because I didn't have time—I got 200-plus emails in the first week—and so I just wrote back and gave him my number and he called. We talked for a long time and dated for 8 ½ months before living together. Online dating is a good way to find out about someone's demographics quickly," she said.

There are thousands of other success stories like Jackie's, which is why singles keep logging on. But despite high-achievers' willingness to give it a try, according to my data, fewer than half—45 percent of single women and 46 percent of single men—said online dating web sites were actually a good way to meet a potential partner.

"In a year and a half online I've never met anyone I wanted to date. I've gone out with 10 to 15 people and talked or emailed with lots of others, but it's like they are the leftovers at the bottom of the barrel," complained Anne, a 30-year-old physician in Boston. She said she might consider a matchmaking service.

Matchmaking services are tapping into the desire to meet eligible singles with a minimal time investment but a substantial monetary one. It's Just Lunch pairs up busy singles for lunch dates in dozens of cities nationwide. Their web site encourages singles to sign up: There are 110 million single adults in the United States, the site notes, but the average 27-year-old has only 11 single friends. It's Just Lunch boasts a 1-in-8 chance that a first date will call you for a second date within 24 hours.

Some seek a combination of online dating and speed dating, a service where singles meet in a structured environment for a short period of time. If, after three minutes, a woman is interested in seeing the man again, she'll make a notation on a scorecard. The man will do the same, and at the end of the evening, the organizers will match up those couples that expressed mutual interest. According to Ken Deckinger, cofounder of HurryDate, an online dating and speed-dating group based in New York City, his clientele are predominantly high-achieving singles. Even unrelated companies are mixing dating information with their larger business messages. Property Shark, a nationwide real estate data provider, has created a "man map" that plots the number of single men by income in various neighborhoods in major American cities. Using U.S. Census data and local topographical maps, the man map graphically plots single men by average income. The red zones are a "meat market" while the pink zones denote the "girls' night out" regions where men aren't residing. The New York City man map was originally created as a present for Kelly Kreth, a publicist for Property Shark who was single and in search of dates, and then became a popular tool on their general web site. While the company doesn't offer any matchmaking services, clients seem to like this clever web tool, and the firm plans to add this man mapping feature in several more cities as data becomes available.

A generation or two ago, dating advice was practically free; mothers and aunts advised daughters and nieces, magazines published articles on how to land a man, and singles generally paired up with someone who lived in their home town. Today, high-achieving women are cash rich and time poor. The advice of old seems a bit out of date for successful SWANS. And a new market has emerged to meet this need.

Advice writers are targeting their wisdom. In their 2005 book, *Closing the Deal: Two Married Guys Take You from Single Miss to Wedded Bliss*, Richard Kirshenbaum and Daniel Rosenberg open with a direct appeal to the "smart, attractive woman with a great sense of humor and a shoe closet to match." In an entire chapter devoted to the successful woman who is also a successful deal closer when it comes to marriage, the two men reassure women that they can be a "sexy, successful postfeminist who knows what she wants and how to get it"—and still get the man.[9]

Kristin Kelly at Match.com advises SWANS to create an "authentic" profile. "Don't overcommunicate and overexpose. Don't compromise. Don't claim to be something you're not. Be real. If you're really looking for a great long-term relationship, it's about connecting with someone who is connecting with the real you." She said women should think back to the last great relationship they had and think about why it worked. In addition, she cautions women not to despair if Mr. Right isn't on the site on the day they sign up. "Sixty thousand new people register on the site each day. If someone isn't there today, come back tomorrow or a week from now. The chances are very high," she said.

In a section on branding, Rachel Greenwald encourages SWANS to play up their intelligence: "A woman whose brand includes 'intellectual' is likely to attract a smart man, or at least a man who appreciates smart women."[10] But she does caution high-achieving women not to come off as "masculine." Short hair, power suits or jackets, and black leather briefcases are a no-no. If you're aggressive at work, that attitude can't come out on dates. "In the end, a man will get to know all of you. Being smart and strategic" means learning how to use your assets at the correct time.[11]

Greenwald also posts her advice online. In a dating advice column on MSN/Match.com, she recently fielded a question from a 43-year-old real estate president seeking advice about how to talk about her career accomplishments on a first date: "I'm very successful in my career and earn a high salary," the woman writes Greenwald. "I have a beautiful loft in a posh downtown neighborhood, wear a fur coat in the winter, vacation at spas and top resorts around the world, and my business card says 'President.'" But despite these material successes, the writer is lonely and wants to meet the right man. "When I go on dates, I am rarely asked for a second, and my friends have told me it's because I intimidate men." While she has dated a variety of men, from CEOs to plumbers and policemen, she has not found someone secure enough to pursue her and wonders how she can find a man who is comfortable with what she has achieved.

Greenwald replied first by asking a blunt and on-target question: "I am wondering if your issue is actually that you 'intimidate' men, or rather that you come across as 'snooty'?" Greenwald warned her that few people like women who "flaunt their status." But, Greenwald continued, it is "common" for successful women to intimidate men with their achievements. To get around this, she advised that successful women should "consider downplaying" their success and job title on first dates, and should talk about mutual interests like movies or pets, not accomplishments at work.

"Try to ease men into seeing the 'strong' you, the 'career' you," Greenwald advised. "Play down your wardrobe at first (nothing says 'I am a Princess' like a fur coat!)." And don't wear "power suits, expensive jewelry, or flashy clothing and accessories that reinforce your monetary status" on a first date.[12]

Among the SWANS, reactions to this advice was mixed: Some wholeheartedly agreed, others sighed in resigned acceptance, and still others got angry at the suggestion that a successful woman should downplay herself on a first date. The most interesting aspect of these reactions is the diversity: There seems to be no consensus on what this real estate president should do.

"That's good advice," said Amy, 42. "I think you have to work with what's out there, and the male ego can be very fragile. Male-female relationships work well when one person takes the lead role. What's interesting now is that that is shifting: Sometimes it's the man and sometimes it's the woman."

Others agreed, though more reluctantly. "I would expect that it's actually pretty practical advice. It's probably not even crazy," said Rebecca, 32. "But I can tell you that most of my women friends— and probably me included—would be disgusted to have to do it."

Still others reacted strongly against the play-it-down strategy. "I'm not comfortable downplaying myself. [Your success is] something you should be proud of. If you have to camouflage it, he's not the right guy. That's a recipe for disaster," said Cynthia, a 34-year-old San Francisco event planner who married shortly after graduating from business school. "I read all those advice books— those books sell, but 99 percent of them are crap. Just be yourself."

So, should this single, 43-year-old president of a real estate company tell men her title on a first date? Can she wear her nice jewelry and expensive clothing from the get-go? Or should she downplay all of these elements to allow men to get to know her for what's on the inside, as Greenwald advises?

It's a debate among friends. Nadia, the anesthesiology resident, made an exasperated face at the idea that the real estate president should downplay her business success. "That's so not fair. Why shouldn't she be proud of her accomplishments?" But Shayna, a fellow resident, seemed more despondent about the advice. "It's practical, but is it right? It's because women learn to compromise. They've been so disappointed that they have to change to get what they want," she said. "In your 20s, you have a hard-core attitude. In your 30s, you freak and want to have kids. Your true personality is in your 20s, and then time and the environment dulls you and you have to change."

Melissa and Kristen, friends since elementary school, took issue with the comments about dressing and speaking in an understated way on a first date. "You have to wear all the bling you can so that they know you like that stuff," said Melissa, laughing but serious. Kristen disagreed: "You should play it down. It's sexier that way. If you put all the coins on the table there's nothing to come out later on. Play yourself down, absolutely, because it's more attractive. People spend their whole lives showing off the biggest and the best. Sometimes the most interesting people are just subtle. It's more enjoyable." "That drives me nuts," said Michelle, mimicking an introductory conversation: "Oh, where did you go to school? A school in Boston. Where in Boston? In Cambridge. Oh . . ."

Whether SWANS are paying dearly for advice or getting it for less from women's magazines, self-help books, web sites, or well-meaning friends, relatives, and manicurists, it's the same chorus: Be more feminine, more subdued, or dress in a certain way. And this drives some successful women to distraction.

Jill, 28, remembers a friend who always complained men were intimidated by her. A mutual friend advised her to be a bit more feminine and flirtatious, rather than constantly talking about power and accomplishments. "Maybe it really does work, but wow, that says a lot."

Raquel, an investment banker, said she's struggling with the femininity question herself. "I'm five-foot-four. I don't have the physique of a guy, so I had to figure out my own angle as a female in a man's world," she said. "In the beginning I repressed my femininity, but not anymore. I don't learn sports talk or try to talk the talk. Some guys aren't used to women in their office, but I'm there and I wear pink. I never wore pink until I started working, and now I wear skirts and pink."

"Maybe it would be better to hold back a little on expressing my opinions and being so blunt. But I haven't tried that yet," said Anne, 30. "I haven't tried to make any changes. But I do naturally tone it down when I just meet someone. I'm less in their face." Heidi, a PhD student in English from Boston, said she puts "graduate student" in her online dating profile but doesn't want to draw attention to her PhD in particular.

"Sometimes I feel like I need to be more muted," said Hope, 30, a marketing executive training for her first marathon. "I can tell if a guy is intimidated. I drive a BMW and if he drives up in a Civic, it can be awkward."

Marcia, 41, said she tries to avoid talking about money, but she admits it's often challenging. "Once they see your house, your car, your jewelry, where you sit at the theater or opera, it becomes apparent." Little things make a difference, she said. Instead of the diamond and sapphire ring she usually wears, or the large pearl stud earrings, on a recent date with a man who she knew made less money she "chose to wear turquoise jewelry to downplay it a little bit."

As for her success intimidating men, Raquel, the 25-year-old from New York, isn't worried. "It's not that I think that as a successful women I'm at a disadvantage, it's more about what I want. I want a lot of things that my friends don't want."

Self-fulfilling Prophecy

Dating expert and author Nancy Slotnick lists "He must be intimidated by my beauty and/or success" in the top five excuses women use to explain why men don't like them. But she doesn't put a whole lot of credibility into this excuse.[13] When "successful, smart women *expect* to intimidate men . . . it becomes a self-fulfilling prophecy," she said.

"It's a really great crutch to think that no one dates me because I have a PhD," said Heidi, a 29-year-old doctoral candidate in Boston. "I think it's all an excuse so you don't feel bad. If you are searching for a reason [that you are single], that's a flattering one," agreed Kathleen, 27, a lawyer from Oklahoma City. "*Sex and the City* girls are supposed to be strong and powerful, but all they talk about is dating. What about Martha or Oprah?"

From Kathleen's experience, men are seeking out intelligent

women, so the idea that high-achievers are at a disadvantage seems laughable. "All the girls I went to law school with are married except one, who has been dating a guy for four years, and I think they'll get engaged soon. This idea that men are intimidated . . . huh? If you talk to my fiancé and his friends they'll have no interest in a Playboy bunny. They are all interested in us because we are smart."

My new data find that although 81 percent of high-achieving single women aren't waiting to get married—they are living their lives to the fullest right now, they report—underneath this optimistic exterior, many women are panicky, and their anxiety doesn't help their chances at finding love.

Cynthia said that the "fatalistic attitude that women have if they aren't married" is like "the plague. It doesn't discriminate, it just wipes everything out. There is a bitterness when it comes to men. 'I'm never going to find him' or 'I don't understand why it never works out.' That attitude feeds more negative interactions, and I wish there was a way to imbue single women with a sense of hope," she said. "If everything else is great, but you don't have a ring on your finger, our society focuses on that, so a lot of those women engage in unhealthy relationships because they want to be with someone, anyone. You'll accept things that you wouldn't accept if you didn't base so much on what other people thought of you."

Julia, a 37-year-old lawyer in New York, agreed. "My single friends and I talk about it quite a bit. At 37 or 38 they are losing hope. They've had long-term relationships that didn't work out, and I don't know how to let them know there are men out there." Julia married at 35 and has watched her single friends become more and more discouraged. They wear drab colors and "aren't pulling themselves together anymore," she said. "My husband says one of them is starting to fade into the woodwork even though she is so beautiful. It's difficult for me to say this, but they need to stop buying into this bad news."

"When I was in college, I thought I was going to be this great martyr type—achieve great things all at the expense of being single," said Ruth, 35. "It didn't have to be that way." Ruth married her boyfriend after she graduated from law school and has a 2-year-old daughter. "This whole idea that it's hard for high-achieving women to meet men is silly. Don't dumb yourself down, it's not good for long-term happiness," she said. "Who does it fool? When do you get to act like yourself again?"

Amy, a 42-year-old single executive, agreed. She said she's quite happy being single, and though she is certain she'll marry someday, she's enjoying the perks of dating now. "I've dated some really interesting people and I've made some wonderful friends. And the fact that I'm not married allows me to meet more successful men, and that can actually help my business interests. Your personal and your business interests can actually complement each other as a single professional woman."

Michele

Michele was sitting in a seminar about interfaith marriage at the young-adult Catholic conference near Seattle that she attended every year. A lay minister was quoting 2 Corinthians 6:14 to underscore that believers and nonbelievers are unequally yoked and would have a more difficult time in marriage.

Michele's mind went back to Dan. It had been four months since the business trip when she and Dan had met at a bar in Denver, and they had kept in touch. When she left Denver, she told Dan that because of their different religious backgrounds—he wasn't practicing any form of religion and she attended church events three times a week or more—they would have to remain just friends. "He was very supportive and asked all sorts of questions about my faith. He basically just didn't go away," she said.

In fact, Dan was coming to visit her in Seattle.

"This was a total conflict for me," Michele said. The influential members in her orthodox parish repeatedly said that they frowned upon dating someone who was not Catholic because it would distract from her faith. "The fact that I hadn't intentionally gone out to find someone didn't make it easier to deal with the guilt, but I knew in my heart that I had not premeditated this course."

Still, Dan came to visit. "Going to visit was a really big deal for me," Dan said. "I never went across the street for anyone else before, let alone got on a plane."

And the two of them had a great time.

"The men I had dated before were often selfish, insecure, and control freaks. They treated me like a commodity and were non-committal. But Dan was totally different," Michele said. "He is content, confident, and kind—and kind was a huge thing for me—and I was beginning to discover that those three qualities lead to a lot of other wonderful things."

Michele said she never had a long checklist of what her ideal man would be like. She wanted to be happy, she wanted a man who would improve her life, not detract from it, and she had always intended that he would be the same religion She added, "It wasn't a big checklist—it wasn't that he had to be six-foot-two and blond or anything like that. I just needed to be true to myself."

So she "went with her gut." Other relationships hadn't made sense, but this one felt right. "You can't tell me that most women dating pricks don't know they are dating pricks. There are signs there, of men who will cheat or are selfish. Do you come equal to their feelings? I should want to give him more than he needs and he should give me more than I need."

And Dan gave so much of himself. "Yes, religion was an issue. I was involved in my church and it's discouraged to date outside of it. But he wouldn't go away. As we got to know each other better, I decided I didn't want him to convert. That wasn't the point. I was in love with him and who he was. He swore that if I stopped participating in my religion, I wouldn't be the same person either," she said.

After his visit to Seattle, the couple exchanged dozens of emails each day, and in one month racked up $100 phone bills for more than 70 hours of talk time to shrink the distance between Colorado and Washington. But six months came and went, and Michele was getting frustrated. She had been downplaying her relationship with Dan, always saying he was "just a friend." Her parents and friends in the church wouldn't approve. And it was getting too difficult. She was doing everything she could to follow the rules and marry within her faith: She'd been going out on dates with many different men in her church, but she couldn't get Dan out of her head.

"I called after we'd known each other for about 11 months and told him that this relationship wasn't going anywhere—and I liked him too much to be friends, so he probably shouldn't call again.

"Still, though, he wouldn't go away. He never went away. That's the moral of the story here. He was very persistent. And then work sent me back to Denver for another few weeks so that I could lead the next batch of training seminars. That's when we both realized it was really happening."

Chapter 4

Gentlemen Prefer Brains

It is a truth universally acknowledged, that a single man
in possession of a good fortune must be in want of a wife.
JANE AUSTEN, *PRIDE AND PREJUDICE* (1813)

JUSTIN IS A 30-YEAR-OLD ASSOCIATE at an international hedge fund in New York City, and he's confused about why his female friends keep complaining to him that men aren't interested in successful women. He and all the guys he knows are looking for a woman who has ambition, drive, and a curiosity about life. How much she earns or where she went to school are secondary; sure, those things can be pluses, but mostly he's looking for a best friend who will share his dreams for the future.

In Justin's ideal world, he'd be able to have dinner with his wife and talk about what's going on at the office—his projects, his career—and ask her about hers in return. He's looking for some back-and-forth discussion, some advice, and a real sense of mutual engagement. "You want them to get it and not just be like 'Yeah, that's my husband, the big business guy,' et cetera," he said.

The intelligence Justin is looking for in a wife is really a curiosity for life. "You want someone who is well educated and someone who uses that education not only to target a professional or career path that is challenging, but also uses that education to pursue any range of intellectual interests." If pressed to make a list of the characteristics he's looking for in a woman, Justin ranks interesting personality, "the right values," and good looks as the top three. "It's about enjoying being with the person, having fun with the person, being challenged by the person." He's looking for a woman who is "ambitious, stimulating, and has a chain of responsibilities just like I do." And he clearly attributes this set of "ideal woman traits" to his upbringing: "My experience on this is probably shaped by my own mother, who went back to work when I was 5 years old and is now CEO of her company.

"What a guy's mom did means a lot about whether he's going to be challenged by his spouse. It's going to be shaped by the attitudes from their own respective backgrounds. I come from a fairly liberal family in that sense, and . . . everyone was expected to have a career and work," Justin said. "Men with successful mothers are going to be interested in successful women," he continues. "My mother loved raising children. She still says it was the best part of her life, but she wasn't going to be relegated to that forever. She had other interests. And that's the kind of woman I'm looking for."

Are men looking for a dependent lass who will attend to their every need? Or just a nice rack and a shapely pair of legs? Maybe men want a woman who just says "Yes, darling" all the time, or perhaps a woman who can't make decisions without them?

SWANS are smart women in many respects, but when these able women buy into gender-based stereotypes of what a man is looking for in a woman, they not only insult the men they are trying to attract, but also give off negative vibes about their own self-confidence.

Any generalization about what men as a group want is bound to be problematic, but there have been some major shifts in men's preferences over the past century—and it's looking good for SWANS.

Since the 1930s, researchers have been asking men what they want in a wife. And my, how times have changed. Whereas today's young man ranks love and attraction as most important, a few generations ago it didn't even make the top three. A dependable, sweet lady who had skills in the kitchen was the prized catch in the 1930s; these days, guys are looking for brains and beauty—and a sizable paycheck seems to sweeten the deal.

Men who were in their 20s in the 1930s, the grandfathers or great-grandfathers of today's SWANS, reported that, first and foremost, they were looking for a wife who had a "dependable character." The ideal wife should be emotionally stable and mature, with a "pleasing disposition." Love and mutual attraction ranked #4 in importance, just a few notches ahead of the desire for a wife to be neat and a good cook. A woman's financial prospects were second to last on the ranking of 18 characteristics, just slightly more important than her political background. That she be intelligent was less important than that she be chaste.

A similar survey, conducted with modern young men in their early 20s circa 1996, found that the rankings had shifted considerably. Love and attraction ranked #1, with dependable character, emotional maturity, and pleasing disposition following in order after that. Education and intelligence shot up in importance to #5—from #11 in 1939—and her financial prospects now ranked as more important than either her chastity, her ability to cook, or her skills at keeping house.[1]

Today men are looking for intelligent, passionate, driven, and fun women—and SWANS are the prime candidates.

As one 35-year-old lawyer said, "I want to marry a woman

---

with a sexy mind, a great sense of humor, a kind heart, and a little spark." If she has a fantastic job and makes a lot of money, most men report, it's a great bonus. Although some admit it gives them pause to think about their wife outshining them in their same line of work, success, power, and prestige are generally aphrodisiacs.

So, though women still think that men are put off by successful girls, the guys say it ain't so. In a recent Match.com poll, 74 percent of women thought men would be intimidated by accomplished SWANS, but a full 62 percent of men said no way: They aren't afraid of dating or marrying career women.[2]

Successful women perceive their assets as liabilities, said sociology professor and author Pepper Schwartz. "Young men see these women growing up: She's your doctor, your teacher, your professor. These models can be quite erotic."[3] And my new national opinion data underscore these assertions:

- Seventy-one percent of high-achieving men said a woman's career or educational success makes her more desirable as a wife.
- 92 percent of men who describe themselves as "successful" or "very successful" say they are *more* attracted to women who are successful in their careers.
- High-achieving men are attracted to women who are as intelligent, accomplished, ambitious, educated, and confident as they are, or more. Eighty-nine percent of high-achieving men report that they'd like to marry, or already have married, a woman who is as intelligent as they are, or more.

Successful, smart men seek to marry successful, smart women. Forget the old saying that opposites attract. Men and women are looking for peers, not superiors or subordinates.

"I am looking for an equal, a partner. Someone who is better than me at certain things and can help me to develop and make me a better individual," said Ian, a business school student in Philadelphia. "Someone who I am able to help and give that person a sense of satisfaction from helping her to grow. Because career, intellect, and education are so important to me, the kind of a person that I am going to spend the rest of my life with needs to be as driven and motivated as I am. I'm really looking for someone who shares my values."

Sociological studies repeatedly find that *like attracts like:* Men who perceive themselves to be smart and successful are attracted to women they perceive to be smart and successful. And they are looking for equals or "best friends," not subordinate women.[4]

"I look to date people who are my peers, who are doing things they care about and are pushing the envelope on it. So for me, whether it's income or degree, however you want to measure success, I don't think I'd have any problem with my partner being equal or better than I am. I just don't agree that for security reasons or male dominance issues that you would marry someone with different aspirations," said Michael, a 26-year-old New Yorker who works in private equity.

Matchmaking groups that pair up couples based on these sorts of interests have had great success. Eric Columbus, a 35-year-old lawyer in Washington, DC, is the founder and director of Friendswap, a free matchmaking service for young professionals. Around Valentine's Day, singles fill out a web-based questionnaire outlining what they are looking for in a significant other, and Columbus and his team make the matches. In the first two years, Friendswap was responsible for eight marriages, with dozens more couples in serious relationships.

Columbus said the men who come to his Friendswap parties are looking for intelligent women with a lot of interests and a good sense of humor—in short, women who match men's perception of themselves. "These professional men see themselves in the phrase

'I am large, I contain multitudes,' and they are looking for a woman who shares their interests and passions," he explained.

At core, both men and women are looking for a partner who makes them feel good, someone to share fun experiences, someone who "gets" them. So SWANS are just as likely to meet their mates as any other women. Many men prioritize intelligence, success, and ambition in a woman, but they are also looking for something more. Does she value our relationship? Do we have fun together? Can we laugh? A woman's accomplishments certainly don't hurt her chances of getting married, but degrees and money alone won't make a man drop down on bended knee.

Although it is true that 46 percent of single high-achieving men would like their future wife to be more attractive than they perceive themselves to be, high-achieving men value those traditionally masculine achievement characteristics as much as they do the more typically feminine qualities. These men envision similarly successful women as also motherly and nurturing, and a full 68 percent believe that smart women make better mothers.

Nick, a 38-year-old New York banker, said that for the past 15 years he has dated "power women," and though success is a bonus, it isn't the main thing he's looking for. "I want to date someone who wants to make time for me—someone who is around to have fun with and really build a relationship," he said. "Women say, you know, look at all the secretaries—they're all married and the lawyers aren't. They say, 'Men are afraid of successful women' or that men aren't attracted to successful women. No! The fact that you work until one o'clock in the morning and on weekends probably has a lot more to do with it. Why would I want to date somebody who's not around? That probably has a lot more to do with it than anything else."

Brian, 31, an investment banker, agreed. The argument that men are intimidated by women who make a lot of money is "too simple an argument to answer a complicated question. It's a safety valve for these women—to boil it down to something so simple and self-gratifying. And the wrong answer distracts you from the right answer. I don't care how much money she makes. Is she a nice person?"

Dating advice writer and seminar leader Christian Carter, founder of CatchHimandKeepHim.com, serves as the weekly online advisor to thousands of women nationwide. In one of his recent blast emails, he warned successful women not to get too caught up in their success; instead, women should keep it real. "A man might enjoy the idea of a woman being successful, but it isn't going to make him think about her like he might a woman who pushes all his male buttons. A man doesn't think, 'Gee, she's got a great job, makes good money, and doesn't depend on anyone else to support her, I think I'll be into her.' "[5]

That said, new data and interviews with high-achieving men nationwide suggest that there are three big reasons why men say they are interested in SWANS: intelligence, self-confidence, and ambition.

INTELLIGENCE "I drive myself intellectually and I think intelligent women are the sexiest women alive. It's very important to me that I marry a smart woman, but there are different types of intelligence. I like the idea of a woman who is independent and who challenges me," said Trevor, a venture capitalist who splits his time between California and Connecticut. "Guys who think they are intelligent and are secure in their success want women who are the same way."

"I'm looking for someone who is deeply engaged in what she does," said Josh, a 29-year-old California entrepreneur. "I'm attracted to different types and kinds of women, but that engagement would have to come from sharpness and intelligence. I want to be kept on my toes."

SELF-CONFIDENCE Out at the local bar, Joseph, a 26-year-old lawyer from Iowa, and his buddies met two women. After chatting them up for a bit, the guys invited the girls out on a group date the following weekend and gave them several options. Would they like to go out for dinner, go to the opera, or join them back at the same bar to watch a college football game and get drunk starting at 9 a.m.? The women, trying to be polite, kept smiling and said all the options sounded good. "They were afraid to express an opinion and it was a real turn-off. Those are very different options! Be yourself and tell us who that is!" said Joseph.

Men are looking for women who make assertions when they have opinions and who have their own options and plans, so they aren't dependent on guys, report dating experts.[6] And the women that Joseph met had blown it. Indeed, according to my new data, 97 percent of single high-achieving men said they would like to marry a woman who is as confident as they perceive themselves to be or more.

AMBITION Kevin, a 27-year-old business school student in southern California, said that it's a "huge turn-on" for a woman to be ambitious and driven. "Ambition in a woman tells me and my guy friends that she's not so much interested in our finances. She's looking for a good person, not a placeholder. Plus, if I'm ambitious and she's ambitious, she'll understand where I'm coming from."

Kevin said he'd been watching a dating reality TV show called *Hooking Up*, where women are interviewed about their dating techniques. "On the show, one girl is a doctor, but she says she's a hairdresser when she goes out to bars. That's a mistake. Being an MD is her best trait—and she should hype that. Be modest, but don't ever try to hide the fact that you have big career aspirations. That's sexy."

Sixty-eight percent of single high-achieving men report that they would like to marry a woman who is as committed to her career as they are to theirs. So if a man senses that a woman doesn't have ambitions for the future, it might send the wrong message about why she's on a date with him.

Dollars and Sense

Conventional wisdom has it that men are intimidated by, or less attracted to, women who make as much money as they do or more. This thinking holds that men prefer the image of the male provider bringing home the bacon to an appreciative wife and children tucked away at home. But times are changing, and high-achieving young men don't perceive salary as an obstacle. For some high-earners, it's a nonissue, and for lower-earners, it's an added plus.

According to Heather Koball's research on male attitudes toward marriage, when men believe in equality and shared roles in a romantic partnership, there is no correlation between income and marriage.[7]

"More often than not I'm dating women who make more money than I do," said Andrew, 30, who earns in the low six figures as a brand marketer. "I've dated doctors, lawyers, and other professional women. That's an attraction, that they were motivated to get those degrees." Plus, Andrew is looking for a woman who can hold her own in the relationship. "I won't like someone because they are good in their career, or make a lot of money, but if she's a great woman, and she has that, it's a real bonus. I'm not looking for someone to take care of."

Indeed, when men are given a choice, as they are when ticking preference boxes on online dating sites, earning good money matters. According to Match.com data, about half of the men surveyed date women who make as much money as they do. And 51 percent of men on their site specified a *minimum* income for the women they were interested in. On another site, 35 percent of male users said they were looking for women with *higher* incomes than their own.[8] And a 2005 Marie Claire/Match.com survey of more than a thousand single men ages 26 to 36 found that 87 percent of respondents think it would be "sexy" to date a woman who earns more money than they do.[9]

As a group, high-achieving single men resoundingly agreed: New survey data from more than 1,600 high-achieving men and women nationwide found that 97 percent of single men would like to marry a woman who is as capable of earning a good income as they perceive themselves to be or more. Plus, 75 percent of married men said their wives were as capable of earning a good income as they are or more.

Still, not all men are comfortable with the shift of power in a relationship if their wife made more money. Kevin said he and his friends had been debating this question recently: "My friends and I argued about it for a while. It's completely silly and irrational and juvenile, but there is still the idea of the male as provider. One friend said he was worried about the woman having more say in decisions if she made more than he did—it was about control. It's about pride and control. Certain guys would feel emasculated. But that part isn't such a big deal to me. If you have two people who are passionate about their careers all the way through, who knows what happens?"

From his living room overlooking San Francisco Bay, Josh, 29, said he has read a lot about society's changing expectations of the gender roles men and women should play in relationships. And, he reflected, the rapid changes have left young men and women confused about what they really want in a partner. "I wouldn't have a problem with my wife making more money than I do. The stereotype is that girls always want to marry up, but that's not necessarily happening anymore, so our conscious and subconscious desires about who we marry are pretty conflicted."

In fact, among high-achievers polled recently, 82 percent of single women and 74 percent of single men said they have a clear, very clear, or extremely clear view of what kinds of qualities and characteristics they are looking for in a spouse. But sometimes that list of qualities can be a bit off: According to my new data, only 50 percent of married respondents said that at the time they met their spouse, he or she matched the image of what they were looking for "exactly" or "a great deal."

Mothers and Sons

Simon, a musician, is married to Daphne, a lawyer. When Simon's father died, his mother, with three kids under the age of 15, got a job and supported the family. In her 60s now, Simon's mother is finishing her PhD in education. Daphne said Simon's mother was an excellent model of a nurturing and ambitious woman, and she believes that is one of the reasons Simon was so attracted to her.

The modern, successful men in their 20s and 30s today are the sons of pioneering generations of high-achieving career women. Their mothers serve as role models for how a woman can be nurturing and successful at the same time. Graham, a political science professor, said his mother met his father as she was finishing her PhD in the 1960s. "If your mother is a success, you don't have any ideas of success and family that exclude a woman working," he said.

My original Harris Interactive survey data finds that 72 percent of mothers of high-achieving men worked outside the home when they had children. Among married high-achieving men, their mom's employment status while they were growing up and wife's current income are significantly related statistically: Men whose mothers were employed were almost twice as likely to marry women who earned $50,000 or more a year as men whose mothers were not employed when they were growing up.

In addition, among married high-achieving men, their mom's education level and their wife's education level are significantly related: 78 percent of men whose mothers had college degrees married women with college degrees, and 19 percent of those men married women with graduate degrees. Of men whose mothers had graduate degrees, 62 percent married women with graduate degrees and 27 percent married women with college degrees.

Among those men whose mothers worked outside the home, 75 percent agreed or strongly agreed with the statement "Men are more attracted to women who are successful in their careers," as opposed to 57 percent of men in the larger survey who said they felt the same way.

"Younger men are much more egalitarian about marriage in general. They grew up with working mothers. Fifty-four million women work and an awful lot of those women are mothers. Their sons aren't looking for *Leave It to Beaver* in their own house," said researcher Randi Minetor, who wrote a book titled *Breadwinner Wives and the Men They Marry.*

Sixty-two percent of high-achieving single men disagreed with the statement "Women who are stay-at-home parents are better mothers than women who work outside the home." Among high-achieving men, 73 percent said they disagreed with the statement "It is usually better for everyone involved if the man is the achiever outside the home and the woman takes care of the home and family."

"My mom worked on Wall Street at a bank for a while and then went to nursing school, which was certainly a professional career for women of her age. After she had four kids, she went back for her BA. I'm very proud of that. I was like, right on, Mom. Now she teaches nursing," said Andrew.

Justin, whom we met earlier in this chapter, said his mother, Lynne, 65, was a role model for him: When he was 5, she went back to work and is now the CEO of her company. "The era that I grew up in had a very different hue of women," she said. "The attitude and expectations of women have changed dramatically: If you were interested in a career, it was going to be a teacher or a nurse. But even those were temporary careers. Now my sons are going to be supportive of whatever choices their wives make."

Two of her sons are married to successful women, and her youngest, Justin, seems well on his way. "Men who value intelligence in a woman aren't unique," Lynne said. "[My sons] have a lot of friends like that as well." What's changed, she adds, is "the idea of what a father's role is. Fathers are really more involved in family life than they were then, and in terms of my sons, they are going to be involved and their attitude toward family life is healthy.

"I'm hoping my son will end up with a woman who has a good attitude toward family life as well. Which is a tall order, yes, but if the person is intelligent and has energy, [she] can always have a career at any point," Lynne said. "I hope they can work through it as a family."

"Marriage means there's one cake," said Jackie, a 30-year-old advertising manager. "Where's the quality of life if you both work 80 hours per week?"

Her husband, David, 34, quit his job as a tax attorney a year into their marriage to write a book and to be, in his words, a "house-husband" who takes care of Jackie.

"Now he's got a bigger slice of the cake, he's got more time, and maybe one day it'll be my turn. But it's all one cake, so him having more time is a net benefit to us," she said. David agreed: In addition to taking care of the house, cooking, and writing, David manages their social calendar. "We have a lot going on. [Our social life] has to be managed pretty actively as well. I make sure she is kept in contact with old business associates of hers in the network and generally support her career. It works."

This, said researcher Randi Minetor, is becoming more common. "While women are able to make a lot more choices about their lives, so are men," she said. "Men can feel more comfortable choosing careers in the arts and research. Men can be small-business owners, run not-for-profit organizations or other things where they aren't going to make a lot of money."

It's Jackie who is bringing in most of the bacon in their house, and David said he's thrilled she's willing and able to take her turn as the provider. When she wants to take a break, either when they have children or when she wants to make a career transition, he'll go back to being a lawyer.

Despite her busy schedule, David knows their relationship is Jackie's #1 priority. When she talks about his career and writing, she uses the words "we" and "us."

David and Jackie met on Match.com. David realized right away that they had a shared sense of values, in addition to that initial attraction. "When I walked her to her car on our first meeting in 2003, I saw she drove a 1998 Ford. Later I found out she has no debt. She makes a good salary. She didn't care about the car she drove and didn't need to be ostentatious about it," David said.

David said he had a very female-influenced childhood. "I never really developed a sense that women couldn't or didn't stand to achieve a lot," he said. One of his sisters has a PhD in psychology and another works on political campaigns. "My mother taught me that women are at least intellectually equal and just as passionate and dogmatic about their career choices as anyone else," he said. And now he and Jackie are supporting each other as a great team.

·　·　·

Joseph, the 26-year-old lawyer in Chicago, has light brown hair, broad shoulders, and frat boy good looks. Raised in Iowa, Joseph went to college on the East Coast, but just as he was graduating, he took a trip back home and met Ashley, a special education teacher with a master's degree. Ashley was two and a half years older than Joe, and she was finished with graduate school while he was just finishing college. Yet the two clicked immediately. "I spent six years on the East Coast and when I finally decided I wanted to get serious, I found the homecoming queen from Iowa," he said, laughing.

Ashley is teaching now and will return for her PhD in the next year or so. Joseph speaks about her research interests knowledgeably and passionately. After four years of dating, the couple will be married soon, and Joseph is clearly proud of his fiancée. "When we met, she had just gotten out of school and was looking forward to working. She would never have allowed a relationship to get in the way of her career. And I'm really supportive of that.

"I work 70 hours a week as a lawyer and make a lot more than she does, but Ashley reverse-commutes to the suburbs. She's up at 5:30 and at work at 7:15 and home by 5 p.m., and she works really hard 180 days of the year."

As the couple look forward to married life, they are having some big-picture conversations about career, family, friends, and life balance. "Ashley brought up a question: What's the most important thing I can do for you when we're married? I said to let me live my life and have the same social interactions we had before we were married," Joseph said. "She said she wanted me to stay focused on the need to put effort into the mutuality of our relationship and the stuff we do together. I know our careers and family life are going to balance out around those goals."

As for advice for single, successful women, Joseph said women should be honest with themselves and the men they date about their accomplishments and goals for the future. "Women should ask themselves if the guy is a person they *want* to spend time with or who they think they *can* spend time with. Be discriminating. And be patient," he said.

Ashley has been a bridesmaid seven times and has four more weddings coming up, Joseph said. "She was no longer making it a secret that she wanted to get married and was ready well before I was, but she was good about it and it was never to the point where it affected our relationship.

"To me, 30 doesn't signal anything. I don't see that it should for women, either, but clearly it does," Joseph mused. "Still, I don't think successful women should feel a sense of urgency or panic. There are plenty of men like me out there!"

"But darling, I just want you to be happy . . ."

Well-intentioned comments from parents and relatives often put a lot of pressure on high-achieving single women. One SWANS said her father blamed her for being "too picky"; the mother of another SWANS used the long drive from their home to business school to express her hope that her daughter would find a husband while she got her degree. "My mom calls every night to ask if I met someone," said a third. "No, Mom, they haven't fallen out of the sky today."

The parents of SWANS want their daughters to be happy, and, quite naturally, parents judge their children's choices and prospects by the benchmarks of their own dating and marriage experiences.

When the mothers of SWANS were in their 20s, smart, successful women were less likely to marry. Most women who were going to marry did so in their early 20s. A 30-plus single woman was considered a spinster. Not so for this generation of high-achieving men and women, for whom it's quite normal for a woman to walk down the aisle for the first time in her early 30s.

Still, mothers worry.

Melissa and Kristen, who grew up just a few blocks from each other, laugh about the comments their parents have made recently. "My best friend just got married, and Melissa and I were in the wedding," said Kristen, 27. "We did pretty much every-thing together growing up and our mothers are best friends. My mom was always asking her to set me up with someone, and I would joke that my mom thought I had a hunchback and a wandering eye because she would come up to my friends and ask if I had talked to any boys. Our family would make jokes about Old Maid Aunty Kristen. It was like I couldn't get a date unless someone helped me. So . . . I started dating Anthony, and now she's like, 'When are you getting married? Do you talk about it? What time of the year would you get married?' Even my dad has gotten in on it," she said.

Kristen said it was very important that her boyfriend get along with her family, but she laughed as she remembered Anthony's first introduction to her father and brother. "They were all going shooting together. So when he was first introduced to them, both my dad and brother had a gun in their hands. No pressure, right?"

My new survey results show that single high-achievers believe that getting married would please their parents—and they feel the pressure. Some 49 percent of high-achieving single women and 57 percent of high-achieving single men say that their parents will be disappointed if they don't get married. Indeed, 15 percent of high-achieving single women and 25 percent of high-achieving single men say that their parents are pressuring them to get married, and 11 percent of SWANS and 19 percent of high-achieving single men say the fact that they aren't married is a source of tension between them and their parents.

The parents of SWANS have high standards for their future son-in-law as well. Seventy-three percent of SWANS said they believe their parents would prefer to see them married to someone who earns at least as much money as their daughter does. And 64 percent said they believe their parents would prefer to see them married to someone who is at least as educated.

Indeed, Alice, 56, hopes that her high-achieving 28-year-old daughter will get married soon. Alice isn't as optimistic about balancing career and family as her daughter seems to be. "What I hope for her professionally is that she will be really passionate about a set of issues and she may want to do doctoral work because it would allow her to gain more control over what she does eventually," said Alice. "Personally I hope she finds someone who she wants to marry and who wants to marry her as soon as possible. It would be nicer to have children without having a lot of difficulty. It's too bad she is single because it puts added pressure on her," Alice said. This pressure has been the source of mother-daughter tension at times. "Sometimes we'll not talk for a week or two. If she's in a bad relationship and not happy, we won't talk because she knows that I won't approve," said Alice.

Mothers, listen up: Your daughter knows that you love her and want her to be happy. She also knows that you are hoping that she'll meet and fall in love with Mr. Right tomorrow. Tell her the first, but not the second. Dating norms have changed since the 1960s. Your successful 30-year-old daughter is not a spinster. Talk to her about these issues using the data from this book. She's a lot more than a statistic to you, but these good news numbers apply to her.

Chapter 5

What SWANS Want

To be so bent on marriage—to pursue a man merely for the sake of a situation—is a sort of thing that shocks me; I cannot understand it. Poverty is a great evil, but to a woman of education and feeling it ought not, it cannot, be the greatest.

—JANE AUSTEN, *THE WATSONS* (C. 1801–1807)

JILL HAD A PICTURE-PERFECT relationship on paper. She had been dating her boyfriend for five years, during which he finished his PhD and then moved to California to be with her while she went to business school. But once at school, she realized that although the relationship might have worked for her in the past, it wasn't what she wanted for the future. "We were very close to getting engaged— like, an hour away. He had the ring. And I had to end it. I said, 'I don't want to feel like this when I get engaged.'" Her family was devastated by her decision, but she knew she'd made the right choice. "He wasn't the person I wanted to marry. There were different things I wanted to do. I was just so panicked at the prospect, even though he was exactly what I thought I was looking for."

Three months later she met her current boyfriend, a lawyer, who had just ended a six-year relationship himself. He's exactly the right match for her for the future—but not at all what she expected. She is white, he is black. "It's not what I'd have envisioned. It's not what I had in mind, but we're so much more similar than we are different. And I'm so happy," she said.

Deborah, a new mother in New York City, said she keeps reminding her single friends to give guys a chance—and think outside the box. "Don't be so picky. You are getting married to a human being with flaws. Relax these standards of perfection that don't exist," she said. "The last guy you went out with, what exactly didn't you like about [him]? I would never have married my husband if I were nit-picking about the things I hear my friends reject guys over."

New York dating coach Nancy Slotnick said her ambitious clients are "looking for a guy who is set in his career—also because this means that he is more likely to be in relationship mode." She added that very few of her clients are put off if a man's success doesn't come with a big paycheck. Nor does a man have to be more aggressive in his pursuit of career success to make successful women swoon.

My new national opinion data bear this out. In terms of earnings, 60 percent of high-achieving women report that they'd like to marry, or already have married, a man who is *equal to them* in terms of ability to earn a good income. Interestingly, fully 25 percent of high-achieving women are seeking a man who is *less* aggressive than they are, and 39 percent said they'd like to marry, or already have married, a man who is *more* easygoing than they are.

Dawn, a 32-year-old black mother of two, said that a few years ago, as a single mother struggling to work and care for her child, she made a one-page list of what she wanted in a man before posting her profile on an online dating site. "And my friend looked at this list and said I was going to be single forever. Was I all the things on that list? Well, no, I'm not."

After she had been promoted to a prestigious management position at her firm and relocated to L.A., she posted an ad with revised criteria: She was looking for someone who was funny, down-to-earth, trustworthy, loyal, blue- or white-collar, nonsmoker over the age of 35. "I originally wanted a guy who goes to the office in a suit, makes six figures, and owns his own house, who doesn't have kids. Instead, I found a man who doesn't wear a suit, doesn't make six figures, doesn't own his own house, and has a child and drama with his ex. But he has the most beautiful sense of humor, he works hard, and I feel protected by him," Dawn said. "If you love someone and think they are your soul mate, none of this other stuff matters. Follow your heart. Don't date no broke man who lives with his mom and can't pay off his Jag. But if he's a teacher, give him a chance."

Marrying Up

From evolutionary biology to the writings of Jane Austen, conventional wisdom suggests that women want to marry men whom society deems to be more and better in every way: a man with more money and education, who is more successful at his job and can support a more affluent and comfortable lifestyle.

Even today, a mother's advice to her daughter has usually been to marry up: to snare a man who has more resources and who will spend those resources so that she and her children will be protected. If a woman does not succeed in this, she runs the risk of poverty or spinsterhood, with no one to take care of her. As Elizabeth's mother admonished in *Pride and Prejudice,* "If you take it into your head to go on refusing every offer of marriage in this way, you will never get a husband at all—and I am sure I do not know who is to maintain you."

Until very recently, this logic made a lot of sense. In 1970, only 6 percent of women over the age of 25 had completed four years of college,[1] fewer than 25 percent of women with children under age 5 were in the workforce, and nearly 80 percent of women had walked down the aisle by age 29.[2] The average woman's life trajectory was fairly clear: graduate from high school, and either marry immediately or attend a few years of college to earn your Mrs. degree.

The man-as-breadwinner, woman-as-stay-at-home-mother family has always been more of a Norman Rockwell idealization than a practical reality. Even in the 1950s, most American families didn't actually fit our idealized images; but when women of that era thought about marriage, they certainly envisioned being with a man who outearned them.[3]

As women have gained ground in both the academy and the professional world, slowly these ingrained stereotypes are being chipped away. For single, educated, and successful women, there has never been more opportunity for equality both professionally and personally. With financial success comes the freedom for a SWANS not to worry who will "maintain" her and the opportunity to marry or not, when she chooses, and whom she sees fit.

Today's SWANS, successful and accomplished young, single women, are much more likely to say they want to marry an equal than to display any urge to marry up. In fact, a growing number of SWANS are choosing to marry complementary mates, men who may not be high-earners or have a string of letters after their name, but who support and enable their successful wife to achieve her fullest potential. Although some critics bemoan the tragedy of these women marrying down, high-achieving women say they are looking for a best friend, not a boss.

Still, there's a long way to go: Studies have repeatedly shown that some women, regardless of their own personal success, still say they are looking for their Prince Charming to come along and whisk them away to a fairytale life. But by ignoring men who may not fit outdated social norms of "suitable mates," SWANS run the risk of missing out on their real storybook romance.

Antoinette

Out with her girlfriends recently, Antoinette announced that she wanted to write a book. "It'll be called, *I Had a Good Time—and I Don't Regret It.*" She proposed a toast to her friends seated around a table at their local bar in Tucson. "Stop and think how far God has brought you," she advised. "I wouldn't do anything differently because there's a lesson in every decision."

Antoinette, a 38-year-old black businesswoman and public speaker, had been dating a new guy for about three months, and she wanted to tell her friends all about him. "His name is Luke, he's 45, and he's a stage designer for the local theater company," she said. "He's white and divorced and has two children," she continued, as her friends' eyebrows went up. In response, she assured her friends that, so far, it seemed like he was most everything on her dream list. "I wanted a guy who was kind, Christian, educated, ambitious, likes to hold hands, tall, and has beautiful teeth. And he's all those things, except the teeth," Antoinette said, smiling.

"Luke doesn't buy me things. But every time I'm with him I feel heard. I feel like he's paying attention. He helps me. Why? Because he cares about me and what's important to me. That hasn't happened with another boyfriend before."

She said she's annoyed by America's cultural perceptions of what makes a relationship a success. "People ask what your boyfriend does. If you say he's an attorney people get all excited. But what if he doesn't call me or treat me well? It's very easy to get caught up in it. The suit doesn't make the man. The media don't say it's OK to be the high-powered corporate woman and date the construction worker. We don't talk about the fact that it's good to have someone who truly loves you."

Luke has a master's degree but isn't a traditional high-earner man. Still, he's not at all intimidated by Antoinette's house, her car, or her various work commitments. Antoinette said she wants to shake the women who believe that their success is holding them back personally: "Everything you've been told about not being able to be successful and have a relationship—it's a lie. And how many times have you perpetuated that lie? It's a self-fulfilling prophecy. Don't be victimized—or victimize yourself. All the men that I know who are men, not boys, want a smart, successful woman."

But she does believe she's had to learn to be two different women rolled into one: a tough cookie in the workplace and melting candy at home. "What helps me in my work doesn't help me in my relationships, but no one tells us that. If we're so busy being high-powered and demanding at home like we are at work, it's just not nice. I have a softer side, and I lose nothing by showing it. I'm not taking the women's movement back because I'm in the kitchen sometimes."

Two of the women having drinks with her that night were also single, so she offered another toast. "Being single isn't a disease. Have a good time." For good measure she added some other kernels of wisdom: "Do not read another book that tells you how to dress or how to date or how men think. You need to burn any books like that. It teaches us to see men as all the same and that's not true. Throw away the list. It works well with your career, but not relationships. If you've been blessed with success, you have an obligation to use it and not hide it—because that's disrespectful."

Evolutionary biologist and author David Buss finds that women prefer to marry men who are more intelligent, financially successful, and stronger—men who will protect them.[4] Social historian Barbara Dafoe Whitehead argues that these preferences make a challenging numbers game for high-achieving women. Educated successful men have more choices of mates because they aren't socially inhibited from marrying women who are considered less successful. The opposite is true for successful women: "High-status women tend to seek husbands of higher levels of education and achievement, and their lofty status decreases the pool of eligible mates."[5]

As more women outnumber men at colleges and graduate school, the numbers just don't add up. In a 2006 *New York Times* column, John Tierney asks, "When there are three women for every two men graduating from college, whom will the third woman marry?"[6]

These gloom-and-doom arguments have penetrated the minds of most Americans—and many SWANS. "Numerically it doesn't work out," complained a 25-year-old investment banker who admits she never lacks for dates. "The smart, successful, attractive girls are looking for smart, successful, attractive guys. But the guys are looking for attractive girls who are good girls for them and they are less bothered by whether or not the girls understand what they do."

As we saw in the previous chapter, most men *do* want a partner who will support them and understand their career goals—just as SWANS want a man who will do the same for them.

My new survey data finds that 76 percent of SWANS would prefer to be married to a man who is as committed to his career as they are to theirs. The idea that women are interested only in more educated or accomplished men is just plain false: Only 15 percent of single and 14 percent of married high-achieving women said they'd prefer a man who is more educated than themselves, and only 23 percent of SWANS and 18 percent of married high-achievers said they'd prefer a man more accomplished than they themselves are.

SWANS date a diverse group of men. A professor in Boston dated a plumber for five months. A SWANS in San Francisco spoke fondly of her relationship with a Yellowstone Park ranger. And a consultant in L.A. said she'd been quite serious about the relationship with her army helicopter nurse boyfriend.

As highly educated young women, SWANS are certainly more likely to date doctors, lawyers, and businessmen than the average woman, but marriage-minded high-achieving women are just as thrilled with their relationships with sommeliers, airline ground crew supervisors, and real estate agents.

Mate Preferences

Women know what they want in a man, but that's not to say that they don't change their minds.

According to the Harris Interactive survey, 82 percent of single women said they have a clear, very clear, or extremely clear view of what kinds of qualities and characteristics they are looking for in a husband. But of married women, only half said their husband matched their image of what they were looking for "exactly" or "a great deal" at the time they met him.

And the changes in national mate preferences during the past 75 years have been even more dramatic. In the 1930s, women ranked emotional stability, dependable character, and ambitiousness as the top three characteristics they were looking for in a man. Attraction and love didn't come in until #5.[7] The women taking this survey in 1939 expected a future in which marriage meant keeping house and child rearing, so they were looking for a partner who would work hard to financially support a growing family.

Practical concerns like dependability and stability outweighed emotional draws like spark and attraction. But most women were looking for a man who had the potential to work hard, not one who necessarily would bring home the big bucks. Even in the 1930s, women weren't ranking a man's financial prospects high on their list of preferences.

Today, women put love at the top of the list, with dependability and emotional stability rounding out the top three characteristics in Mr. Right. While education and intelligence has become more important to women over the years, moving from #9 in 1939 to #5 in 1996, love has moved from #5 to #1.

CHARACTERISTIC	WOMEN'S PREFERENCE	
	Rank in 1939	*Rank in 1996*
Emotional Stability/Maturity	1	3
Dependable Character	2	2
Ambition/Industriousness	3	7
Pleasing Disposition	4	4
Mutual Attraction/Love	5	1
Good Heath	6	9
Desire for Home/Children	7	6
Refinement/Neatness	8	12
Education/Intelligence	9	5
Chastity	10	17
Sociability	11	8
Similar Educational Background	12	10
Good Financial Prospect	13	11
Similar Religious Background	14	14
Favorable Social Status	15	15

Good Cook/Housekeeper 16	16
Good Looks 17	13
Similar Political Background 18	18

In surveys in the 1960s, half to three-quarters of women in their early 20s reported that they would marry someone they weren't in love with if all other desired characteristics were there.[8] Because many women planned to depend on their husband for income, a man's professional status, income, and family background might very well outweigh love. But by the 1990s, fewer than 10 percent of women said they'd marry someone without love. Why the drastic change of opinion?

One explanation is that as women themselves gained access to power, education, and money, they could shift their focus in choice of a partner away from economic considerations and toward love and attraction. Several studies support this idea.[9]

In every field there are SWANS, young women striving to succeed and searching to find the right match in their career and personal lives. SWANS like Heather, a 30-year-old blond-haired green-eyed firecracker, excel at so many careers and enjoy getting to know so many different kinds of guys that it takes some time, and some exploring, to figure it out. Heather went from being pre-med in college to acing the LSATs and going on to law school and a white-shoe firm. But after less than two years, she quit and now writes for men's magazines and freelances for television sports broadcasts.

Like her career choices, Heather has dated different kinds of men, searching for the best match. Her parents have a specific idea of the kind of man she should be with: around 35; owns his own business; tall, dark, and handsome; intelligent and witty. "I'm like, that's great, but I don't date those kinds of guys," she said.

Her last boyfriend came pretty close: He was 35 and an Emmy award–winning producer. Her current boyfriend is a 25-year-old actor who didn't finish college. "I definitely date every type of guy. Depending on what kind of job I've done, I meet different people. These guys would never get along with each other. They couldn't be more different," she said.

Women who go to bars to search for men with a certain type of diploma or career need to reprioritize, Heather said. "If you want one of these guys to like you as opposed to someone else, stop treating them as if they need a certain pedigree or that they aren't deserving of talking to you. You worry that they feel intimidated by you? You make them feel that way. Be open to the fact that just because you do this career and know a lot about it, there's a lot about life you don't know."

Heather said she's not interested in the guys who look good on paper, and her bold personality just doesn't attract the insecure types. She's looking for someone fun. "I should be with some guy with a vast vocabulary who is very smart. I might be in those kinds of careers, but that's not my personality. It's weird how people immediately put you in that role and tell you what you want. My boyfriend is fun, he's smart, but he hasn't gone through years of school. He wanted to pursue acting. And you can tell—he doesn't have that background and it never ever once bothered me. But for everyone else, that's what they see."

Marriage-minded SWANS are looking for supportive, motivated, and intelligent partners who "just click" with their values and their view of the world. Some SWANS want a team player; others want a natural-born leader. Apathy is a deal breaker, but passion—for a career or calling, and for the relationship—is a must.

A SWANS in Washington, DC, said she dates the "secrets": the shy, artistic kind of guys other women don't recognize as great. A SWANS in San Francisco was looking for a man who matched her sense of adventure. She knew her boyfriend was the one when, after a 45-hour first date, they both admitted to wanderlust: She wants to live in a different city every two years, and he shares her love of exploration and travel.

Melanie, a 26-year-old business school student, mostly dates men who complement her: artists, musicians, and creative, sensitive men who encourage her nonprofit business side. "I need a partner, someone who is on the same team with me. I picture my future husband as someone who will grow more confident as he ages—we'll grow together. We'd be going places, as a team, together."

Kristen, a 27-year-old who works 12-hour days as an investment banker, is dating a vintner who is doing an apprenticeship at a wine import business he hopes to one day take over. Kristen said she's looking for an ambitious, hard worker who knows how to get what he wants—and her boyfriend, who currently doesn't make much money, fits the bill. "He's very motivated to make something of his life, and that's attractive," she said. Her best friend from childhood, Melissa, agreed that mutual support and motivation are key ingredients to her successful relationship as well. "My boyfriend tells me about his day when I get home, and he wants me to be interested. He likes it that I understand what he's saying. He includes me in his day and wants me involved. That's really important."

High-achieving women are looking for men who will be good parents, who are attractive and smart. But Mr. Perfect doesn't need to have advanced degrees or a big income to make them happy. My new survey data reveal that 92 percent of high-achieving women would like to marry, or already have married, a man who is likely to be a good parent. Only 14 percent of SWANS said they were looking for a more attractive man; 80 percent of high-achieving women report that they'd like to marry, or already have married, a man who is *as* attractive as they are. And 73 percent of high-achieving women report that they'd like to marry, or already have married, a man who is *as* intelligent as they are.

SWANS repeatedly mention intelligence as an attractive quality in a man, but that intelligence comes in different packages for different women. A 28-year-old management consultant in Los Angeles said she's attracted to "guys who know stuff." Her concept of intelligence has less to do with the letters on his résumé and more to do with his ability to "read obscure stuff and call BS on me." Darcy, a 30-year-old commercial real estate consultant in Chicago, said she wants to meet a man who is quick, sharp, and has a "blue-collar personality" that would enable them to communicate "on the same wavelength."

When SWANS describe their ideal man, they are, in effect, describing themselves. An athletic medical doctor in Boston said she is looking for a man who can play soccer, run, bike, and swim with her. Though she's looking for an intelligent man, it's "not necessarily Ivy League smart" that turns her on. He should be driven, but mellow. Just like her. Melanie, the business student who lives in Washington, DC, said she's often wondered what it would be like to date herself—someone who is driven, opinionated, and, in her estimation, down to earth. "I think I'd really like it," she said.

Most high-achieving women are looking for equal partners. And life balance, a shared sense of humor, and a big heart are more important than money or success. Two Los Angeles marketing coworkers likened the equality they were seeking to pillars of a house, which need to be at the same level for the structure to stand securely. For Madeline, a 31-year-old first-generation Vietnamese American, the four pillars are emotional, spiritual, financial, and psychological. For Lola, a 29-year-old who moved to California from Puerto Rico as a child, it's about balance and passion and a strong commitment to family. "It's a guy's personality that is so important. Someone who can make me laugh. Silly is good," Lola said, laughing herself. Both women had married young and divorced after less than three years. Lola continued with the house analogy as she described the type of man she was looking for: "It's like buying a house. The first house you buy, you can compromise on some things you can't afford, like an extra bedroom or a garage. But the second time around, I'm not willing to lose the garage anymore."

Inevitably, the list of Mr. Perfect characteristics includes a few less noble demands, as well. Younger SWANS have their fair share of picky or petty wishes in their mates: a man who doesn't talk so *slowly;* a certain type of social personality so she doesn't have to "babysit"; a guy who likes puppies, is six-foot-four and buff, doesn't want to play golf or video games or gamble more than twice a month, likes the same music . . . The list goes on.

Often these lists change with time and maturity—and love softens discussions from earnings reports to emotions and passion. "I was much vainer in college. I would only go for tall men. I didn't even look at a guy below six feet, and I'm five-foot-five," said Alexis, a 35-year-old lawyer in San Francisco. "Now kindness and humility have overtaken tall and athletic. I'd like to be with a man who is passionate about something other than [himself], someone with a sense of integrity."

Christina

Waiting for her boyfriend to arrive at the quiet bar downtown, Christina felt exhausted. She was sick of the New York club scene. She'd eaten too much sushi and dated too many of the wrong guys. In the past year and a half, she'd turned 30, been dumped by the investment banker boyfriend, and turned 31. Along the way, she'd wallowed for months in her friends' warning that she was "too much" for men: too much of a challenge, too smart, and too successful.

Two months ago she'd met a tall, blond southern gentleman

who ticked every box on her dream-man list. Tonight, she was going to dump him.

Sipping her white wine, she watched three women clustered at the bar, gossiping. At a nearby table a couple was holding hands and gazing into each other's eyes. Or so it seemed to Christina, who was getting more and more frustrated with her dating experiences.

She was doing well at work and had earned a promotion. But recently Christina had come to a realization: Her friends were wrong. It wasn't her job that was holding her back; the guys she'd been dating were jerks.

"I finally woke up. I wanted to go back and tell [them], and everyone else, that it was nonsense. Anybody who tells you that a guy loves you so much, but he can't handle you and can't be with you is smoking crack. Guys want to be with you if they are into you, and if they don't, they're not. I had to stop listening to this 'I'm too smart' crap.

"They were obsessed with men, just obsessed," she said. "Finally I told one of them that she had a sick obsession with finding a guy and was doing anything necessary to keep a guy or to get a guy's attention. It was so tough to listen to these successful, smart, independent, good-looking women who were better off than most people complaining about how their life was miserable just because they didn't have a man. So I took a break from it."

And after that break was the southern gentleman, who, on cue, was walking into the bar. He kissed her as if there was nothing wrong. Christina smiled wearily. Because he lived in Alabama and she in New York, they didn't get to spend a lot of time together, so it had taken her a few months to figure out that he was a jerk. When she came to visit him, he'd hang out with his friends and ignore her. When he came to visit her, he'd make passes at her girlfriends.

Yes, he acted in all the right ways when he thought someone was looking, and yes, he certainly matched her list for an ideal man. Within the first half hour of their first date, he'd told her he had a law degree (tick!), a passion for politics (tick!), and was a big fan of the southern football conference and played football himself in college (tick and tick!).

After she finished her speech about why things weren't working out, Christina said she felt a weight had been lifted off her. "Thank God I put that list together and I met the guy who fit every quality on the list. He had the law degree, he played football in college . . . he lived in Alabama. Basically I realized he was perfect on paper and I hated him. And it was my lesson in not putting together a list of attributes. From then on I was like, 'He just has to be nice.'"

The choices that SWANS are offered may be a double-edged sword: Follow your heart, and if you want to be in a serious relationship, choose to make it work. Yet with so many options in their 20s and 30s, many SWANS feel overwhelmed. "One of the things we suffer from is that we have so many choices," said Kama, a Chicago-based businesswoman. "We're waiting for something better to come along. We don't want 99 percent of the choices we have." Lindsay, a 38-year-old college professor, reminds herself that she has "agency" over her life—she's in charge—and "that means the 'I haven't met the right person' line is nonsense. I wasn't looking. I've met him five times. There were so many 'right people' along the way, but I didn't choose them.

"Saying I haven't met the right person shifts the blame away from me, when really I have agency. Every morning you wake up and have the opportunity to write the novel. There are only two things you have to do: You have to write the novel and you have to be the star. But you choose it. I'm writing a really great story and I don't have a costar. Why? Because I didn't choose to write one in.

As soon as there's a casting call, people will show up. It's our choice." She paused. "I wonder why I made that choice, though. Maybe because I thought I wouldn't get to be a big enough star if I wrote someone else in? But being a big star is lonely."

After college, Lindsay worked as a teacher for several years before going back for her master's in education, worked for another five years, and then began her doctorate. She entered her PhD program at 30 and finished at 37. Though she dated a lot through her 30s, she said she was in a "suspended place of preadulthood." If there was talk about marriage, kids, and family, Lindsay wasn't listening. "I didn't get the memo because I didn't have a mailbox."

When we spoke, Lindsay had recently ended a five-month relationship with a hunky Israeli plumber. He'd done a service call at her house and she realized that was what she was looking for: a Jewish guy who could fix things. "He was so into what I did. It wasn't about competition. He knew how to fix things around the house and we were impressed with each other. One partner shouldn't begrudge the other partner." The relationship finally ended, she said, because the contrast was too stark. But, she said, "It made me rethink what an intellectual partnership really is."

Lindsay said she doesn't have a list of what she wants in a guy. She isn't picky about height or career, but now she won't date someone for more than a month unless there's a possibility that he's "the one." On J-Date, the online Jewish dating site where Lindsay has her profile, she lists her occupation as "English teacher" and tries to reply to everyone who writes. "An artist would be great, and money doesn't really matter since it's hard for a guy to make less money than I do. Mostly, I'm looking for someone with a story to tell."

Women who are too picky don't really want to get married, Lindsay said, citing examples of several of her friends. "I have a friend who has gone on 100 first dates. The guys aren't tall enough, funny enough, et cetera for her. She just doesn't want to find the right guy. There's got to be some compromise, otherwise you don't want to be married." A few years earlier, another friend was on a mission to get married. "We'd go into a bar to get a drink and she'd scan the room and then say that we were leaving. I just wanted to get a drink, but she was looking for dates." This frustrated Lindsay at the time, but she conceded that it worked: "She did it. She married a great guy."

Now Lindsay is taking the same attitude: "Women who are high-achieving work really hard and like control. We think we can make it work. If I work really hard on my doctorate I'll get it. And now I can work really hard on finding a husband. Maybe. I'm thinking of putting 'find a husband' on my to-do list, just so I make it a priority. I'll put it on my calendar," she laughed. "It's my choice."

Marrying Down

As women climb the corporate ladder and garner more graduate and professional degrees than ever before, the media have been harping on the fact that these successful women may be forced to marry down because there aren't enough available and interested men of equal caliber.

According to the most recent Current Population Survey data, a woman with an advanced degree is more likely to marry a man with an advanced degree than a woman who does not have similar education. And the same is true for women who earn a good salary. A woman's earning power has become a more important determinant, over time, of a husband's expected future earnings. The more money a single woman earns, the more likely she is to marry a man with greater future earning potential.[10]

But prestigious jobs and earning power also offer women a

choice: SWANS can date and marry for love, support, and all the other intangibles that couples say makes a marriage fulfilling.

The argument that successful women may be forced to marry down is insulting on several levels. First, it's insulting to young women who have been fed a message of social equality for decades. Until recently, the crisis was that women weren't being treated equally in the education and work worlds. Many pioneering women stepped up to the challenge and broke through glass ceilings so that young women in the 21st century could excel in education and the professional world. Now, the crisis is that women are overeducated? It's either too little or too much; in this argument, women can't win.

Second, it means that, as a society, we judge a person's worth solely on his or her earning potential. "Lesser" and "lower" men are defined as men who don't have a particular pedigree or a job of suitable prestige and income, rather than making any judgments based on a man's character or ability to emotionally support a family. Not only does this argument ignore the personality and caring potential of men in favor of a paycheck, but it completely devalues caretaking work—the work that women have been doing in the home for centuries. Feminist groups are often the ones that complain the loudest about their daughters' inability to find a suitable man. It's hypocritical and elitist for feminists to complain that successful women are having to marry "below their station." No one ever complained when high-achieving men married women who had less education or income. So why should it be a crisis when the reverse is true?

Not all feminists have gotten on this misguided bandwagon. Wendy McElroy said she is outraged by talk that there is a marriage crisis for successful women. After she attended a conference where several women spoke about the dire situation they believed their daughters faced as they continued on their ascension to the top, she wrote, "There is a 'marriage crisis' only for women and in-laws who demand an attorney or doctor for a husband and do not wish to welcome a plumber or mechanic into the family."[11] For Lindsay, and many other SWANS, this isn't an issue. But not all women have embraced this equality.

"We'll reach true equality when you hear a bunch of women sitting around at brunch saying to each other, 'No husband of mine is going to work,'" said David, a 40-year-old teacher. "That sounds crazy, doesn't it? But for a certain group of men, you can hear them saying that all the time about their wife or future wife. You never hear women say it. Hopefully, though, we're not that far away."

Women may be bigger culprits of this snobbery than men: Whereas men are increasingly open to marrying women who make more money, hold more prestigious jobs, or have a fancier degree, women, studies find, are slower to embrace this element of equality.

"We are seeing more and more women with men who make less. We all have to change our outdated notion of what a man is and a woman is and not limit ourselves or our partners to these definitions, and realize that life is fluid. You should really be looking at your scenario as 'Who does it make sense for to stay home with our child,'" said Carolyn, 36, who said this kind of thinking hurt her in her last relationship. "We're so stupidly status-conscious, we are worried what people will think—or we are worried what we think ourselves. 'If my husband stays home, what does that mean? Is he a pansy? What does that mean about me?'"

SWANS are more likely to be comfortable outearning their spouse—as long as the spouse is working in some capacity—especially if it means he is pursuing a career about which he is passionate. One doctor talks about her crush on a male nurse she works with: "If only he were straight." Another SWANS said her fiancé, a starting-out entrepreneur, "just smelled right," and money wasn't an issue.

"I dated an investment banker. He was financially well off but miserable," said Angela, a 31-year-old who works in advertising. "I've also dated an unemployed guy who was happy, but broke up with him because he didn't do anything, ever. There's practical reasons why you have to make money, but as long as the guy is striving, it doesn't matter."

Alexis, a lawyer, agreed: "I'd marry a man who made less money, absolutely. My job affords me the opportunity to do that—to not care about it. I'm cautious of ne'er-do-wells who might sponge off of me, but for someone who doesn't have a good job, that's a concern for other women, but not me," she said. "In most of my relationships I've made more money and it's never been an issue that's come to the surface. We've shared expenses."

The pressure to pay the bills is ever present, and SWANS who anticipate taking on most of the burden themselves said they don't feel prepared to take on that pressure alone. "I struggle with the idea of being the sole breadwinner. It's the typical fear: Can I provide for my family?" worried Kama, a successful 28-year-old management consultant. "If he makes less money, that's OK—but where is the upside of his career? Could he start a business on the side?" she said, pointing out several nontraditional but lucrative ways to earn money.

For 42-year-old Carrie and her family, the fact that she outearns her husband has allowed them to split the care of their 5-year-old daughter and enables her to pursue her business career. "I've usually made more money than he does. And he was like, 'You go, girl.' He was very supportive of my career and my success," she said of her husband, a real estate agent who is 13 years her senior. "He had been through it all himself and could envision what was coming next for me."

When Carrie was consulting from home while her daughter was a baby, she made about 30 percent more than her husband. Now that she is back at a large company, she is earning six times as much as he does. His flexible schedule allows him to pick their daughter up from school each day and spend the afternoon with her. And her income allows their daughter to go to a private school. "It doesn't bother him that I make more money, but it does put the burden of responsibility on me. I just can't say 'I'm too stressed out—I quit.'"

At 35, Jessica is an executive at a large New York City financial company, just coming off a string of late nights on a major restructuring project. But at 6 p.m. on a Tuesday in July, she was wearing a frilly skirt and a tank top with her shoulder-length brown hair pulled back in a tight ponytail. Leaving the world of corporate finance behind, she focused her mind on her personal life.

"My dating experiences have been excellent. I'll go out to play softball and then go out to dinner with some of the guys I meet and things grow from there. There's always a commonality and I've been treated very well. The thing is, though, I'm looking for the right person. I'm not going to complain about someone's socks. My God, I don't even care if *my* socks match. But if he's not the right person, and I look down and notice his socks, that'll be the headline of the brunch story with my friends."

Two years after college, Jessica married her boyfriend of four years. But less than a year into the marriage, he became abusive. She had been accepted to business school, and right before classes began, the physical and verbal abuse hit its peak, and she left him. Her mother, a devout and conservative Catholic, argued that Jessica should return to her husband and make the marriage work. In a matter of weeks, Jessica was disowned from her family, separated from her husband, and faced with enormous business school loans.

After her first difficult year of business school, she found a job in New York. She was 25 and divorced, but she had survived a tough period on her own. "I woke up one morning and said, 'Wow, I love it here. I can do this, I can live and make it through life.' I've never looked back."

A decade later, Jessica has had dozens of boyfriends, just no one that she felt was quite right. She's dated millionaires and artists and said she's looking for someone who is ambitious, self-aware, and curious. "I like the idea of a best friend. Clearly someone who I'm attracted to, don't get me wrong, but I just want to laugh with someone, that's all."

Are you a zero without the plus-one?

SWANS are women who have achieved a lot and aspire to even more. SWANS are smart, successful, and ambitious women. And yet many SWANS feel they aren't complete without a man, or ask themselves, as Sex and the City's Carrie Bradshaw does, "Why does one minus a 'plus-one' feel like it adds up to zero?"[12]

Some SWANS worry that marriage has become another goal they must attain, another award for success. "Even if you have a graduate degree or two and a high salary, there's this notion that you're not a woman until you are married," said Cynthia, 35.

For high-achieving women, is getting married just another item on the to-do list?

Melanie, a 26-year-old business school student, said that when she lived in California she didn't feel pressure from her friends to get married. But in business school, she's feeling more anxiety. "The tipping point comes hard and fast." Now she's joined an online dating web site and is making finding a husband more of a priority. Still, she wonders how much of this is desire to have a great relationship and how much is the pressure that she's putting on herself to live up to expectations of how her life should be.

Patricia, 32, said she gets angry when her girlfriends appear to be on a mission to get married and get the job done. She said these women aren't really interested in love, they are interested in keeping up with society's expectations. "Marriage is not some box to check off, like getting your degrees, because it can be unchecked.

"Those women who are desperate to get married scare me. Some women ask, 'Could I marry this guy' as a first question. I ask, 'What does this guy's CD collection look like?'" she said. One of her friends, a 27-year-old professional woman, is on a mission to get married, and Patricia doesn't know what to make of her determination. "I guess that's what the majority of people do. But there aren't the same goals and achievement posts [for a relationship]—not like law school and careers. You can't set the same goals."

And men can sense when a woman is treating marriage like another agenda item. Christian, a 36-year-old single entrepreneur in Washington, DC, said he's been on dates where he wanted to ask, "'What is the purpose of getting married? You want to have a spouse you are proud of? To be loved?' People get married for all sorts of reasons, many of which stem from insecurity. If you see marriage as a success rung, can it be accomplished by your usual calculus? There are different boxes we want to tick to make us feel more secure," he said.

Nick, a 38-year-old businessman in New York, said women with an accelerated agenda and time line scare him. "If you're a man and you want to get married, you want to meet somebody who wants to get married, too. But most men want to be chosen for themselves—for the person they are, and the two of you get along and playing on the same team and all that stuff, not because you are like a sperm donor and a paycheck and somebody to cut the lawn," he said. "If she's got a checklist you don't want to be like 'Okay, if I get more than six Xs on this list of 10 or 11 things I'm going to marry the guy.' Nobody wants to be that kind. You want to be somebody who she genuinely wants to be with."

Getting married is not about a diamond ring or the beautiful white dress. It's not about what your parents or friends or colleagues think about you. It's not about checking a box on the list of life experiences. It's about sharing a life with someone—and it's hard work even under the best of circumstances. Settling for a "he'll do" kind of guy isn't something that should be on the table for intelligent SWANS. That's not to say that a happy marriage shouldn't be a goal. But it's a different kind of effort from, say, your graduate school application or landing that corner-office job.

Dawn, a 32-year-old married high-achiever with two children, said she recognized this early on. "If I stuck with the list of things I wanted in a man, I wouldn't be married. The things that make you strong in your career or great in your company aren't what a man wants in a date—and we're so busy! Saying to a guy that you can fit him in between 5:30 and 6:30 isn't sexy," she said.

But, Dawn continued, it's not that she didn't follow her dreams—she did. And after relaxing the time line, she's happy with what she accomplished. "When I graduated from grade school, around age 13, I wanted to be a doctor, have two kids and a husband, and be making six figures—all by 23. So, around 23, I was like, hmmm, no. But if you put it at the 20-year mark, around 33, I think I'm doing pretty good."

Envisioning a future that relies on the desires of another person is challenging for ambitious women who are used to controlling their own destiny. Most SWANS said that at 15, they expected to be married with children before their 25th birthday. And though few have accomplished that goal, most said plans are made to be revised.

"Ten years ago I wanted to get married at 26 or 27. Now, 31 or 32 would be nice, but it's completely out of my control," said Heidi, 29. "When you get married older, your time line gets quicker. If I get married at 32, how long am I going to wait for kids? It puts stress on the relationship. The converse is that as you get older you know what you want. And that's a real benefit," she said.

"I thought I'd be married by now," said Kristen, 27. "My mom got married when she was 20. I thought 27 was so old, and I still think it's so old, and we thought we'd be married ladies who lunch and have babies by 30." But, she said, she wouldn't change a thing. "If a woman right out of college came to me and asked me what she should do, I would tell her to find a career that you enjoy and that challenges you—but where you can get out of the office by six or seven so you can go out to dinner with friends, go on fun dates, but still be challenged during the day. You need that balance. But enjoy your 20s, and forget all that stuff about being married with kids by 25. Explore and enjoy."

Chapter 6

Who Is Mr. Right?

SMART, SUCCESSFUL WOMEN have all their options open. If a woman can support herself and is educated and accomplished enough to hold her own, finding a man is the quest for a complement. SWANS are thinking outside the box.

"Women have earning power, so they're less intent on finding a husband who is a high earner and more interested in finding someone who is an all-around good partner," said Stephanie Coontz, director of research at the Council on Contemporary Families and author of *Marriage, a History.*[1] Dating coach Nancy Slotnick tells her clients that to think outside the box doesn't mean "settling," it just means taking an honest look at what *really* matters in a mate. "Women have different criteria for what they want for a proactive search versus if they just meet someone," Slotnick said. "So they wouldn't reject some guy who didn't have such-and-such degree if they met him in a bar and thought he was cute and nice, but when they do an online search or tell me what they are looking for in a man, it's a much higher standard. This means that you are using criteria as an excuse. Just get out there."

So once the list goes out the window, who is Mr. Right? There's the older man, secure in his career and encouraging of the young high-achieving woman. There's the younger man, impressed by a SWANS's success and full of energy and adventure. There's the complementary match, a nonalpha male who wants to support and enable the career of the high-achieving woman. And, of course, there's the artist, the creative genius who provides the most romantic of the foils for the go-getter, achievement-oriented, Type-A woman. High-achieving women are increasingly open to nontraditional options as they search for their perfect match across age, race, and religious groups.

The Older Man

New Harris Interactive data find that 83 percent of high-achieving women would consider marrying a man who is 10 years older than they are. SWANS describe men as "one life-stage behind" women in terms of maturity and readiness to marry and start a family. So a man at least five years older would be an ideal match. "Older guys recognize that if you are confident and know what you want, they'll get what they want," said Kama, a 28-year-old management consultant who has dated men up to 13 years her senior.

It's common to see couples in which the man is a few years older than the woman. In fact, it's so common that when many demographers talk about how many eligible men there are for every 100 women, "eligible" usually means men a few years older. So, for example, the statistics would reflect the number of men ages 30 to 34 for every 100 women in the 25 to 29 age group.[2]

SWANS in their 20s and early 30s describe older men as more confident than men their own age, and believe that the extra maturity and self-knowledge that comes with age is an attractive quality. "It's refreshing to date someone who is older. And they understand how to treat a woman," said Madeline, 31.

"Older men understand themselves better. Experience tells them that they need something more than 'Look how hot she is.' They are looking for someone who is intellectually compatible, because they are more secure," said Raquel, a 25-year-old investment banker. Jody, a 31-year-old postdoctoral researcher, agreed. "Guys are immature, and it's difficult to find a mature, age-matched counterpart," she said. "The guys I'm usually interested in are in their mid-30s to early 50s."

Nationally, about 20 percent of married men are six or more year older than their wives.[3] It's a classic setup: The older man has more money, more power, and more prestige than his younger male counterparts because he is further along in his career. And SWANS are attracted to his self-confidence and experience. It's unlikely that a man in his late 40s would feel competitive with a woman 15 years his junior, so the older man is described as thoughtful, supportive, and encouraging of a successful, up-and-coming woman.

Older men might be more likely to settle down and get married, some SWANS muse, but getting the right man at the right age often seems tricky. "Men under the age of 33 are not targeted in their dating," said Jessica, 35, who has dated men in their 30s, 40s, and 50s. "Between 33 and 43, it's 'Oh my God, what have I been doing, I need to make an acquisition and get on with my life.' They want to buy you," she laughed. "Above that they are old enough to be super secure and they are looking more for companionship."

Marcia, a 41-year-old from San Francisco, added that men in that late 30s–early 40s bracket might be searching for a certain (younger) type of woman. "There's that type of successful man who at 35 or 40 wants to get married—and they want a 30-year-old. So if you want that type of guy, you need to know that by age 30. And they want thin women, who have perfect dress and grooming—and even at 30 I was never that." Gloria, a 25-year-old practicing Mormon, said she usually dates older men because men her own age are "floundering around." Her last boyfriend was 42. "And he was successful, single, and normal. He had a good sense of direction."

Vera, a high-powered New York SWANS in her late 20s, met her boyfriend at law school. Both she and her boyfriend are establishing their careers—his in Louisiana and hers in New York—and wondering what's going to happen in the future. Will she leave her network of friends and her new job and join him down South, or will he uproot the company that he started to either move to New York or meet her halfway? "I wish he were five years older," Vera said, adding that if he were a bit further along in his career there would be a lot more flexibility. But her friend Sarah chimed in that age doesn't always overcome distance. Her last boyfriend was 13 years older and lived in Washington, DC. Despite how set he was in his career, the relationship recently fizzled.

Along with more life experience, older men often come with more baggage. Never married and over 40? SWANS begin to wonder what makes the guy damaged goods. "Sure, I'd date a guy who was six or eight years older," said Heidi, a 29-year-old PhD student in Boston. "But after 40, I'd start to wonder why [he isn't] married yet." Marcia, 41, said she'd prefer to date a man in his 40s or 50s who had been married rather than one who had remained single. "They have fewer relationship issues and tend to be more comfortable with intimacy," she said, admitting that as a 41-year-old who had never married herself, perhaps she shouldn't be so critical of others who had made similar choices.

Divorced men may come with alimony payments, a tense relationship with an ex-wife, complicated arrangements with children, and a slew of other hurdles. But for Marcia, these are manageable. Although she prefers the widowers to the divorcés, because it is "easier from the kids' standpoint" if the relationship progresses, Marcia has dated her fair share of divorced men as well. Recognizing how matter-of-factly she was discussing complex and emotional issues, Marcia sighed. "Five or 10 years ago I wouldn't have said all this, but from my experience, it's true."

Amy, a 42-year-old business executive, said she likes dating older men because their "egos are in place." But, she added, "the challenge is that many of them have already gotten married, had kids, they are divorced. They've lived that life and now they just want to be single and free, so they kind of want to see you once or twice a week and that's it. They don't want to develop a more serious attachment where it's weekends and activities and things like that, and that can be heartbreaking if you really want to have a relationship. You have to find men that are emotionally available for that kind of relationship." Amy spoke from experience: Her last relationship was with a man 11 years her senior who had been previously married. The two were together for eight years, including a four-year engagement, before Amy decided he would never actually remarry. Newly single at 39, Amy sought the advice of a matchmaker. She told the matchmaker she was willing to date a man up to 20 years older. "And she said, 'Look, I don't think you need to go more than 10 years older.' And she introduced me to a man about eight years older." That relationship lasted only six months, but Amy said she continues to use matchmakers as a way to get introductions to older men.

"My mother would like me to date a younger man, though," Amy said. "Her concern is that if you marry an older man you'll be taking care of him as opposed to having a fulfilling marriage for a number of years." But Amy isn't concerned about that. "Most of the men that I date have more energy than I do. Actually, one of my acquaintances, she's 45, . . . just married a 72-year-old man. He's 27 years older, divorced, successful. She had just dated a number of men in New York and she finally settled down with a 72-year-old. Now that's a bit of a stretch."

Pausing, she thinks about her own dating experiences and laughs. "I do have one admirer, and he is 27 years older. But that's the oldest. He sends the most beautiful flowers and takes me to the most beautiful dinners. And we actually, intellectually, share a tremendous amount in common. He loves giving me ideas around building my business. He is a fascinating person. He's a very successful businessman. So it actually has been beneficial for me to date someone like that."

The Younger Man

When it comes to younger guys, SWANS in their 20s and early 30s are more hesitant. The older man offers stability; the younger man offers virility and adventure, but SWANS aren't as interested in those characteristics. A younger man is still in flux—moving for new opportunities in different cities, perhaps not willing to get serious about a relationship. For successful women with an eye on marriage and family, a man who is still making major life decisions isn't an appealing long-term prospect.

Still, an increasing number of women are giving it a try. Jennifer, 28, can tell you precisely how long she's been dating her boyfriend. "One year and eight months next week," she said. The couple met as graduate students in Washington, DC, when they were both doing internships. A little more than a year ago, he moved to South America to spend a year working as a human rights lawyer. He arrived home yesterday, and Jennifer is concerned about the future. "He's two years younger than I am, and I don't know if he's ready to settle down. I feel the anxiety, and now it's this big thing. It's always present. We've had conversations about marriage—that I brought up—about whether he is showing the kind of commitment I need. He sees marriage as a black hole: It scares him. He does feel closer to that step, but he's not saying he definitely wants to marry me. I just want to see more concrete signs," she said. "I could wait four or five years if I knew we were getting married. It would help if he were a bit older."

Her friend Sarah sympathized. "Before I dated the older guy, I dated a guy who is two years younger, and we worked on [a political] campaign together. We were together a lot, but he moved to Europe." He took the next step in his fledgling career, and his relationship with Sarah wasn't at a stage where the couple even thought about discussing the long-distance possibilities.

Yet, older SWANS are more open to the possibility of building a relationship with a younger man. Fifty-five percent of single high-achieving women ages 35 to 40 said they would be open to marrying a man 10 years younger, according to my new survey data. For women in their late 30s, a man in his early 30s might be a real possibility. But many women worry that it's the men who aren't taking them seriously as marriage potential because of the age difference.

Jessica, 35, said she has several friends who see younger men as "a feather in their cap." But, she added, it's mostly a sexual relationship rather than one with longer-term potential. Alexis, a 35-year-old California lawyer, says men "significantly older and significantly younger" are interested in her, but not men her own age. "In their 40s and 50s, and 25 years old, sure, they are eager," she said. "My guy friends say that the older guys aren't intimidated because they've been there and done that, and the young guys aren't intimidated because [they don't] know any better. I'll take it on because it makes me feel better, but I'm not sure that's the case."

Susan, a 38-year-old saleswoman, said she had similar experiences. At age 37, she decided to "dedicate herself to dating": She got good photos taken and posted a personals ad on AmericanSingles.com. "I was dating like crazy. I had lunch dates, dinner dates—all on the weekends. I had six or seven guys casually going at once. I didn't go out with a guy who didn't want to go out with me again," she said. "And yes, amazingly enough, they were five to 10 years older or 10 years younger. But guys my own age weren't interested."

The Complementary Match

During the weekly wine hour that her law firm hosted for lawyers and support staff, Daphne had been chatting with a handsome man who worked in the file room. She was a young associate, working 60 to 80 hours a week and most weekends, and she had a lot of legal research to do in the file room. "Really, I did!" she said, smiling.

Simon was a year older than Daphne, and had a master's in philosophy. But his passion was music. He had started a band, and the job at the law firm was just paying the bills. Daphne was captivated. "We have two very different sets of friends and we don't necessarily fit comfortably in each other's worlds," she said. She described "the lawyers versus the cool musician types" and confessed that she thinks his friends are "way cooler than I could ever hope to be."

And yet, her interest grew. The two had been dating for a month when she realized it was serious and felt she needed to let the firm know that she was dating one of her colleagues. "I told the leader of my practice area—and she was a very scary woman to me at the time. I mean, here I was, a young associate, telling her I was dating the long-haired file clerk. I was terrified." The two women sat in silence after Daphne told her about her interest in Simon. "And then she said, 'This is a very 90s issue. If it were reversed, I'd say you'd be out of your mind.' She was quiet again and then said I was a very thoughtful person. And finally [she] said, 'You need to leave my office. I'll ask you if I have any more questions.' I thought I was fired."

A year went by and she and Simon continued to date. In that first year, Daphne said she thought a lot about money; she earned more than double his salary. "I was used to traditional dating, where the man paid, but he was more relaxed. We'd go dutch and choose places that worked for both of us." As the couple looked to the future, Daphne said she was grateful that her success allowed her to choose a man she loved, despite his finances. "I can choose from a wider array of men and I don't need to worry about if they can support me. Women can choose partners who will fulfill them emotionally."

When Daphne and Simon got married, the scary boss received an invitation, and she was delighted to attend the wedding. After 11 years of marriage, Simon is still pursuing music, and Daphne is rising in the ranks as an in-house lawyer at a large company. "I dated other men who could have given me money, security, and all the things a woman 'should' look for in a man. But I was looking for someone creative, loving, emotional, and demonstrative. Whether he wore a suit to work and made a lot of money just wasn't as important."

Couples like Daphne and Simon are becoming increasingly common in the United States. According to my new data, 33 percent of high-achieving married women said they married someone who didn't earn as much money as they did at the time of their marriage; 67 percent of high-achieving women reported that they would be comfortable being the primary earner for their families; and 82 percent of single women said they would be willing to marry someone who earns less money.

The concept of a male breadwinner is still a powerful social construct, but slowly and quietly, the realities are beginning to shift. More than half of married women who earn $55,000 a year or more are married to men who earn less. Indeed, even at the highest income brackets, there are signs that high-earning women are seeking complementary matches: In 2000 some 75 percent of Fortune 500 female executives outearned their spouse.[4]

As women earn more graduate degrees than men, it's not surprising to hear that many women are marrying men with fewer letters after their names. Some 84 percent of single women said they would be willing to marry someone who has less education, and 54 percent of married women said they married someone who had less education than they did. This doesn't mean that women are marrying men who are less intelligent or have less ability to be successful. But it does demonstrate that high-achieving women aren't limiting themselves to an arbitrarily small group of men: These women are using their resources to find a man who is the best match for them, not someone who simply looks good on paper. In fact, high-achieving women are casting a wider net than the average woman: Only 72 percent of non-high-achieving women said they would be open to marrying a man who had less education, compared with 34 percent of SWANS.

Successful men and women aren't immune from the money tensions that so many Americans face. In one national survey, 50 percent of all respondents said that money, and specifically the money spent on personal purchases, was a source of tension in their relationship.[5] Among high-achievers, it's a similar story: 50 percent of married high-achieving women and 46 percent of married high-achieving men reported that money is or has been a source of tension in their relationships.

Cynthia, a 34-year-old black event planner, is married to Sam, a stock trader. He has a law degree but does not practice, and she has a business degree. Cynthia said she makes more money than her husband, and always has. Sam quit his job and followed Cynthia to business school. He proposed at the end of her first year of school, and the couple was married right after she graduated. But during their engagement, Sam was unemployed. "That was hard," Cynthia said. "My parents picked up the lion's share of the wedding, but it was difficult on his ego."

The couple live in California, and Sam works market hours: He is up early and home by 2 p.m. "He does all the cooking, all the laundry. I work longer hours than he does since I'm building my business." Recently, there's been some tension. "He's been saying that I don't respect him, and it's not true—but perhaps I need to show that more. He provides emotional support and he's really good around the house. It's a challenge. There are times when I can't handle it, but there are times when I realize he loves me so much that it's OK."

Money tensions among high-achieving couples are often the result of insufficient communication and honesty about each partner's perception of marriage, said Randi Minetor, author of *Breadwinner Wives and the Men They Marry*. In her book, Minetor has a chapter titled "Single and Successful: Could You Marry a Man Who Makes Less?" She asks several penetrating questions about a woman's perception of the "natural order" of the family relationship, about money, and about the concept of being a working mother. "She needs to think about what her expectations are about raising children as the higher-earning partner in the relationship. Is she comfortable with day care? Is her husband going to be willing to be sharing the burden of child care? That's the killer issue in the end."

Among Minetor's most penetrating questions: For a high-achieving woman dating a man who earns less money, how important is an expensive engagement ring? "If having that big diamond, that big reward, is so important, perhaps you aren't cut out to be a breadwinner wife," said Minetor. "I can't tell you how many high-achieving women are offended by that statement. To an awful lot of women, they waited their whole lives to get that ring. Even though they make double what their fiancé does, it's the outward display of what a great catch they got. To expect that from a man who makes less than you do is not about jewelry, it's about status."

Minetor said this is proof that the Cinderella Complex, a concept popularized by author Colette Dowling in her early 1980s book, *The Cinderella Complex: Women's Hidden Fear of Independence*, is alive and well—even among high-earning, high-achieving modern young women. According to Dowling, women, no matter how successful or accomplished in their own right, are looking for a fairy godmother and Prince Charming to "rescue" them from their daily toil. A quarter-century later, the phrase still resonates. "No matter how much money we make, we still think we have to marry up," said Minetor. "There's a sense that I have reached this pinnacle of my career and I have to find a mate that is up here, too, or better. Women were still getting this 'marry up' message from their own parents, and their friends. They would be as crass as to say 'Why would you marry that bum?' Even the most progressive, most feminist group of women—our parents—are saying these things. It's the wrong message."

The first question Minetor got when she spoke at universities was "Are men going to be turned off by me?" "I always told them, the right men will think your success is great. It's a matter of finding the right man," she said. "Because we're geared to marry up, we go for the top guys, and they are going to be the worst at this kind of relationship. You've got to look outside the boardroom. Do volunteer work in the arts, the nonprofit world, and this will expose you to terrific high-achieving men, some of whom won't be earners."

Mr. Perfect: The Artist

As a graduate student, my advisor would often point to the dismal 1980s and 1990s data about the low marriage rates among well-educated women and offer me a bit of personal advice: Marry an artist, he said. The artist's creative enterprise exists on an entirely different level from advanced degrees and the competition of the business world, so there would be less chance for direct competition between us.[6] He'd never be intimidated by my success, and I would always be somewhat in awe of his creative genius. It became a standing bit of humor amid our research: The graduate work was going well for me, but how was I doing in my search for the artist?

A SWANS who was finishing her PhD said she'd be open to marrying an artist, as long as he was "career-focused." A consultant said she would be open to a creative man, as long as he was successful in his field and "really loves what [he is] doing and is good at it." Still, she said that match might be "a stretch" for someone as business-oriented as she is. When high-achieving women think about their future, an artistic man who earns little money and operates in a different creative world seems a bit foreign . . . yet enticing.

Hope, a 30-year-old marketing executive in Los Angeles, said she's dated musicians and artists, and initially the relationships have been fantastic. "It's great because they are so different, but it eventually drives me crazy. They don't understand what I do. Initially I'm attracted to them because they force me to be balanced and free and fun. But I couldn't imagine having them as the head of my household." Recently she dated a musician and felt as if she was always badgering him about his work. "I said, 'What's the plan to get this piece out?' and I was always pressuring him to get a time line for completion, when it seems that creating a piece of music is a lifetime journey for them. We just were thinking differently," she said.

Other women have yet to find their artist and are excited by the prospect. Gloria, 25, said she's ready to date some men who aren't Type-A personalities. "If you date really smart men, they come with their mess. They are overbalanced in one way—and a mess in others. Great at work, bad at dating," she said. Lindsay, the 38-year-old Boston professor, said what a man does or how much he makes wasn't really something she worried about.

Still, there are some very real financial pressures in a partnership where one person's wages are much less stable. Elaine, a 42-year-old journalist in New York, described her four-year relationship with a man who was in communications and trying to break into photography. "He was curious, loved museums, we had similar cultural views—but he wasn't as far along in his career," she said. "He was very financially dependent on me and acted like he was entitled to my money." The two almost got married, but she ended the relationship shortly before they got engaged. "I didn't want to be taking care of him."

Nadia an anesthesiology resident at a New York hospital, agreed: She dated a bouncer at a club she used to hang out at. "He wanted me to be super successful so I could take care of him," she laughed. "He wasn't intimidated by my job, he was excited by it. If a guy doesn't earn as much, that's fine, but he needs to *do* something," she said. Her friend Shayna, a doctor, has been dating a bodybuilder for two years and considers him an artist of sorts. "He wants to stay home, cook and clean and support me. I can see myself with him forever. He understands the demands of my job," she said. Currently he's studying to become an actuary. Because he comes from a wealthy family, she said, he has a more relaxed attitude about work.

There's certainly something catchy about the Type-A achiever pairing up with the artistic type. Even billboard advertisements got in the act in 2005: "Tell your mom you're marrying an artist," advised one placard in the Citigroup *Live Richly* campaign.[7]

Race

Antoinette

As they approached their first Christmas together, Luke told Antoinette that he didn't like the holiday, that it was too commercial and that he didn't want presents. Antoinette said she respected his wishes, but she was too "excited that I have a boyfriend I can buy stuff for" to ignore presents entirely, so during the month of December, she bought various presents. "I would just come home from work and just have clothes for him with me, but no, we weren't going to do Christmas. I didn't even get a tree," she said.

On Christmas Eve, Antoinette was taking a nap on the couch when Luke asked her to go to the store to get some coffee for them. She complained that she was tired, but at his insistence, she got up and went shopping. "And when I came back, he had bought me a tree . . . and decorated it. And he built me a shelf that's big enough to hold 40 pairs of shoes for my closet. I was just stunned," she said. "He's crying, I'm crying—he did this by hand. He could have gone to buy it, but he made it—he sanded it. It's beautiful.

"Then he said there is something from Santa under the tree. Under the tree there's a skillet. I had a cast-iron skillet that I got at a flea market and I dropped it and the handle broke. That was early in our relationship. He found a place that makes them, the old-fashioned kind, and it was perfect.

"He continues to be kind and to see my needs and remember things, and knows what I like and don't like. He pays attention to me," she said of her boyfriend of seven months.

As she sat watching the lights twinkle on the tree, Antoinette thanked God for bringing her such a wonderful man—even if he didn't quite come in the packaging that she'd expected. "Luke and I never talk about the fact that he's white and I'm black. It's a nonissue for us. What comes into play is other people's reactions about us," she said.

On Antoinette's 39th birthday, she and Luke were shopping for a new jacket for Luke to wear out that evening. In the men's section, Luke was browsing through the jackets on the rack. Next to him was a black man doing the same thing. The two men were laughing at something a salesperson had just said. Antoinette came up behind Luke, holding another jacket she had found, and said, "Sweetie, what about this?"

"The black man looks over and sees me and smiles, and then he looks at Paul, and he loses his smile and he walks away. That experience is not uncommon," she said. "Black men don't like the idea of me dating a white man."

Both Antoinette and Luke have dated outside their race before. "From day one, I knew that he was genuine and he wasn't looking at me as some sweet hot black mamma, some fantasy about how good I was in bed," she said.

Other reactions have been positive, Antoinette said. Luke is a stage designer at a local theater that recently put on a production with an all-black cast. At the closing party, Luke introduced Antoinette to the cast. "This black man, one of the percussionists, says 'I knew you had some soul in you. I should have known you had a black girlfriend.' Luke and I laughed," she said.

Luke's parents have been supportive of his relationship with Antoinette. "There isn't a family member who doesn't like me, but oftentimes I get the *30* questions—more than the normal girl would get. Are my parents married? What is my education? I learn to share with people that my mother has a PhD and my father is a minister and that I own my own house and I have a master's degree. And then it becomes OK. But I do have to more or less prove myself as the girlfriend. But when they realize that I'm probably dating down, it becomes OK," she said, laughing.

Antoinette's parents are welcoming of Luke as well. "The expectation is still the same. He's still expected to treat me well, that's not going to change," she said. "And he has to believe in God." Antoinette attends a mixed-race Baptist church in Tucson. Luke is Catholic, but the couple pray together and talk about the importance of religion in their lives. "I pray that one day he does come to my church. It doesn't matter the race. I call it a small country church. It's people who are regular and take care of each other. All of my white friends who have come to my church absolutely love it. When you come and your heart is heavy and you get hugged by someone who is happy to see you, when you come into that space and people are friendly and kind and the music is uplifting," race doesn't matter, she said.

"We've got our differences, but when we are together, it just all works," said Antoinette. "He gets me."

Some 5 percent of all U.S. marriages are interracial marriages—more than 2 million couples, according to U.S. Census statistics—and almost half a million of those are between blacks and whites.[8] Generally, the more educated a person is, the more likely he or she is to be in an interracial marriage. This is especially true for educated Latinos and Asians, whose intermarriage rates with whites has been steadily increasing.[9]

According to the 2000 Census, the last large-scale survey that captured national intermarriage patterns, in 73 percent of black-white marriages, the husband is black and the wife is white, and in 75 percent of Asian-white couples, the husband is white and the wife is Asian.[10] And there's evidence that the number of interracial marriages will increase: According to a recent nationwide poll in *USA Today,* 60 percent of U.S. teens have dated outside their race.[11]

For high-achievers who identify with an ethnic or racial minority, finding a man who is attractive, intelligent, interested, and of the same background becomes significantly more difficult.

Raquel, a 25-year-old Indian investment banker, said she is pulled between her traditional Indian family and her modern New York City life. When she meets a new man, she said, he will often "get caught between what he thinks of as the standard that a girl should be, what he sees in me, and what he wants to believe about me." Kama, a 28-year-old Indian woman in Chicago, said she feels similar tensions. "I have short hair. I talk back to people. I'm not your standard Indian bride." Kama went to a top college and business school. She said she was pushed by her family to be "aggressive, independent, and assertive," but now she's finding that "most Indian men can't handle that." Her older sister recently married an Indian man, and Kama said her mother desperately wants her to follow suit. As she gets older, Kama said, her mother is now saying that an interracial marriage is an acceptable option. "The pressure on me went from marrying an Indian to just getting married."

"Every slice narrows the pie. Education, race, religion—it's a small pool," said Shayna, the East Indian anesthesiology resident in New York City. Her parents want her to marry an Indian man for cultural and religious reasons. Instead, she's been dating an Italian Catholic bodybuilder for the past two years. But as he's not Hindu, she hasn't yet told her parents about the relationship, and because of his ethnicity, she's always got her eye open for someone who will be more pleasing to her parents. "We're pretty serious, but I've always said if an Indian guy comes along, it's the end of him."

Black SWANS said they are aware that the numbers aren't in their favor. Black women are increasingly more educated than black men. According to one survey, there were 166 black women enrolled in college for every 100 men.[12] "With education, it's important—I appreciate it—but the difference between me and someone who hasn't got a degree is that I had the opportunity," said Antoinette.

Though reliable data are difficult to find, much of the good news afforded to white SWANS has yet to benefit black women. And successful black women are feeling the frustration. Adrianna, a black dentist, said that when she lived in Maryland she was never in want of black men to date. Now that she lives in Tucson, she's reevaluating her desire to date only within her race, especially as she sees many of her friends, including Antoinette, in thriving interracial relationships. Adrianna believes that white men are more supportive of a black woman's success. "In the home, the black man provides and the woman shouldn't have to work," she said. "It's a pride thing: Black men don't want to date high-achieving women."

But other black SWANS disagree: Cynthia, a black SWANS in California, said she dated "across the spectrum" and married a black man. "My husband is African American, and the men I tend to be most attracted to are black, but I've dated Asian, white, Indian, Jewish, Irish, Italian, Spanish, the list goes on," she said. Although she felt it was "damn near impossible" to meet a black man with the same type of earning potential she has, she was able to find a man who respected and appreciated her success. "As an African American woman, you reach a point where you reshuffle your list. It changes more rapidly for African American women because the pool is smaller," she said.

Jody, a black 31-year-old postdoctoral researcher, said race hasn't been an issue for her in dating. Generally, she said, she meets only white men. "Given my education and experience, most of the guys I'm going to meet are Caucasian. Socially and politically, I'm aligned with the left, so this all makes sense." Her current love interest is white, and she said it was distance, not race, that was keeping them apart.

Because educated black men are scarce, black women often complain when a black man dates a white woman. Jill, a white 28-year-old business school grad, is dating a black lawyer. In her mind, "there's nothing weird about it. There are so few guys in New York who are educated, nice, get along with my friends, so it doesn't matter that he's black. Of course, my mother says, 'It's so sad you have such a narrow pool to choose from.' " Jill said this relationship isn't what she'd envisioned, but as a couple they are so much more similar than they are different. Her mother, Allison, 60, said she supports her daughter's choice, but is concerned about how other people will react if the couple marries: "It's fine when you live in Brooklyn. When you live in a little town in Tennessee, you'll run into more problems."

Religion

For SWANS already feeling disadvantaged in the dating market, finding a man who shares their religious tradition sometimes seems like an unnecessary burden. If faith is peripheral—relegated to the occasional Sunday Mass, high holy days, or family celebrations—most high-achieving men and women say shared religion is nice, but rarely a deal breaker.

My new survey data find that 74 percent of single high-achieving women and 77 percent of single high-achieving men would be willing to marry someone of a different religious background or faith. Of married high-achievers, 37 percent of women and 41 percent of men said they married someone of a different faith.

Rebecca, 32, said she is looking for a Jewish man because the commonality of faith is comfortable for her. "I think it's a nice thing to share with somebody who occupies such an important place in your life. It's nice to have that as a common factor." Yet she often dates men who are not Jewish or don't believe in God at all. "Interestingly, I find it harder to be with people who are nonbelievers . . . who are agnostic or atheist, as opposed to some other religion. Because it's easier to explain how your faith is different from theirs than it is to explain the concept of faith."

Interfaith marriage is quite common: According to the 2001 American Religious Identification Survey, more than 28 million American married or otherwise "coupled" adults live in a mixed-religion household. Some 23 percent of Catholics have intermarried, 33 percent of Protestants, 27 percent of Jews, and 21 percent of Muslims.[13]

High-achieving men are finding it challenging as well—and they seem willing to compromise. "It's not easy being a Catholic in the New York City financial world," said Andrew, a 30-year-old Jesuit-educated asset management executive. "I'm looking for a smart woman with a strong sense of family, the importance of education, and a good sense of humor. Being Catholic would be a plus, but it's really difficult to find everything."

"I always thought I'd marry someone Jewish," said Zoe, a 29-year-old corporate lawyer who was raised Jewish but doesn't practice regularly. "My husband isn't Jewish. But he's even more than I could have thought of in so many other ways: He's caring, sensitive, intelligent, and isn't afraid of a strong woman!" she said, laughing. "You've got to be open-minded. I don't think there's always one type of guy out there."

Julia, 37, said she similarly decided to look for a "spiritual base" in a man, rather than insist on finding someone in her specific denomination. When she married her husband, Harry, at the age of 35, the two decided to switch off churches: On one Sunday the couple might attend her liberal Episcopalian church, and the next week worship at his more conservative parish.

When faith is a central, guiding force, it shapes and changes the dating life of high-achieving men and women and creates added challenges for successful women who have delayed marriage as they pursue their career.

Mary, a 33-year-old evangelical Christian, ministers to single women in a small parish in Houston and said that she chose to work with unmarried women in their 20s and 30s because she knows how it feels to be a "fish out of water amid all these families in church." Mary often meets with women who are anxious and frustrated by their marital status: "I tell them it's about God's plan for you. Your life is not a failure if you aren't married. Don't be paralyzed by this."

In college, Mary earned a degree in dental hygiene because it was the "safe thing" to learn a useful trade. In her late 20s, she decided to pursue her master's in theology, and by 30, she and six girlfriends—three doctors, a lawyer, a professor, and an accountant—were meeting regularly to support each other as they struggled to keep their faith strong as single, educated Christian women. "All of my girlfriends have advanced degrees, and we weren't meeting guys who were interested in us in our 20s. There were times of disillusionment, but we were just praying for God to work. And now, just a few years later, out of the seven of us in my original group, all but two are married."

Mary said she and her girlfriends bonded over their frustrations. "Well-meaning people around us would tell us we were intimidating to men. We just didn't think that was the case. What bonded us was a spiritual perspective—we were just going to continue to do what we were called to do." Now, she said, she knows that remaining single until 33 was God's plan for her. "Having been single and not getting married until my 30s gives me a voice with women. I gain a hearing with these girls because I was single for as long as I was."

Sometimes it is the network within a strong religious community that brings a couple together.

Jeff, a 47-year-old Orthodox Jewish divorced father of two, lived in Providence, Rhode Island, and worked as a corporate headhunter. It had been several years since his marriage ended, and he was looking to remarry. He put his business skills to work on his personal life: He decided to conduct a search for a wife just as he would search for a CEO for any company. He closed down his business and kept on two staffers to help. He assessed the population of Orthodox Jews in the United States. How many potential women would he have to meet to feel that he'd canvassed the options? Back-of-the-envelope calculations estimated that there were 6 million Jews in the United States, 3 million women, 6 percent of whom were Orthodox. So, 180,000. Of those, he decided only 1 in 1,000 would be willing to move to Boston. Jeff needed to meet 180 women to feel he'd gotten a handle on the market. He called all the synagogues and built a database of 280 names of matchmakers nationwide. He created a job description for this ideal woman, and a profile of himself, complete with professional photos. Then he sent gifts to all the matchmakers along with his introductory packet.

Cut to Naomi, a 38-year-old self-described sports freak living in New Jersey. Naomi was the first person in her family to attend college and graduated a year early. She worked on marketing for World Cup Soccer championships and men's professional tennis. She earned her MBA by putting herself through business school at night and landed a job overseeing marketing for the Olympics.

Naomi's career drive left little room to think about anything else. "I went for the career, the master's, the traveling, and I never really thought about marriage. I mean, I thought I would get married eventually, but it was never an agenda item for me." Over the years, she said, she's been in and out of relationships and had never made a commitment. The pool of eligible Orthodox Jewish men shrank quickly as she got older. "I never said to myself, 'Oh, I'm putting off having a family.' I was very ambitious and I knew what I wanted. So that's why the family and the husband thing was totally secondary. It wasn't even on my mind."

Still, she was well-connected in the Orthodox community, so when Jeff's packet hit the matchmakers' desks, the women instantly thought of Naomi. "All the matchmakers he met in New Jersey said he had to meet me because they were personally friends with me," said Naomi, who was not registered on any of the Jewish dating web sites or officially linked to any of the matchmakers. "I was just friendly with these ladies and they pressed me to go out with this guy who lives in Providence. I really didn't want to do it, but he called and we made a date."

When she met Jeff, it didn't look good. In fact, it was a horrible first date. Naomi said she had come straight from work and was in "power mode." "We schmoozed for a while, but his assessment was that I was a cross between a pit bull and a linebacker. And I had a dinner appointment, so it was short. I wasn't really interested either," she said.

As is the custom, Naomi and Jeff both had to explain to the matchmaker why the date didn't work out. "The matchmaker convinced me to give him another chance. I was dating someone else—and I was also date number 2 of 35 for [Jeff]. He wasn't interested in me and called back the matchmaker for other women, but she forced it and said she wasn't giving him any more names until he went out with me again."

The second date went better because the pressure was off. And the following week they went out again. "After two dates he said 'I'm really starting to fall for you.' He was really old-fashioned and courting me. Women don't allow men to be men a lot of the time. Women are much too aggressive. I was taken aback." She didn't know what to make of this. This man was eight years older, lived several states away, and was *headhunting* a wife. But he seemed so sincere. "I recruited a couple of friends and my mom as my coaches. I couldn't handle it. It was so hard for me to receive the gift that he had to give. With their help, I decided this was real. I had never had someone who was a real man like him."

As Jeff and Naomi continued to date, he was still juggling six or seven other women—and Naomi said she certainly "wasn't drooling over him. I wasn't giving him any signs. I was just taking my time to get to know him.

"I went in and out of relationships and never made a commitment," she said of her dating experiences. "I felt like, when he comes along, he comes along. I was beginning to realize that you can be so successful, but there are character traits that we all carry that unless you are with another person they will never be actualized."

She began to tell herself to open up and make space for someone else to come in. "I was successful and great, and everyone knew that, but I needed to allow a man to give to me. To be needed. Give it a chance. Throw the list out the window. You should only have a few things on your list. Mine was that he had to be a mensch."

After two decades of building a successful career, Naomi was coming to a realization that yes, "I'm great, and everyone knows that. I can make some space for someone and still have a career. But if I was defined by my career, that would be a big sign of insecurity," she said.

Naomi and Jeff married within a year of their first date, and they are living in Boston with Jeff's teenage son. "Personal life success means passion for something. And when you are able to give that passion back, your success multiplies forever," Naomi said. "How many degrees you have just isn't important. Money comes and goes, so you have to look at a person. A lot of people say a certain age is too old or too young, but that's just a number. Be open-minded," she said. "And the rest is all about timing."

Among the challenges for devoutly religious SWANS is sex: If successful women are more likely to marry in their later 20s and early 30s, that's a long time to remain chaste. It's an issue that young adults don't often want to talk about—especially when it comes to perceptions of chastity and success. Mary said she and her girlfriends often prayed for the strength to keep their thoughts pure, and Gloria, a 25-year-old Mormon designed with an Ivy League pedigree, calls her vow to be chaste until marriage "another filter" when it comes to potential dates.

Christian, 36, said he's looking for a woman who has deep faith, intellectual curiosity, humility, and a big heart. As the son of a minister and a missionary, he lives in a different world: He's a tech entrepreneur in Washington, DC, and said he doesn't like to wear his faith on his sleeve—but is certainly looking for a religious, and chaste, woman as his wife. He also realizes it's a "narrow segment" of women who are high-achievers and share his faith and values. "I'd prefer to marry a PhD who is brilliant. That would be a bonus. Wow, we'd have great conversations." But he wonders if it will ever happen.

In some cases, SWANS feel that their faith dictates that they remain single. Petra, 35, was raised in Ecuador, converted to the Church of Latter-Day Saints when she was 12, and moved to the United States at 16. She attended Brigham Young University, where "everyone talked about marriage, but my family wanted me to study and achieve." Out of college and working in San Francisco as a top-level sales executive, Petra realizes it's tough to meet a good match. "Mormon men date Caucasian women. As a single, Latina

Mormon, it's hard, but if it happens, it happens." She said she still has hope: "My boss got married at 39—to a guy she met while she was having dinner alone at a restaurant. There's something inside of me that says it will come when I least expect, if it's meant to be. That's where faith comes in."

Michele

Michele had just returned from her second trip to Denver in a year, and from a very intense three-week visit with Dan, her boyfriend that none of her friends knew about. She was 34 years old, a devout Catholic, and lived in Seattle. Dan was 32, not religious at all, and lived in Denver. This was never going to work, Michele thought.

That night Michele confided in her two closest friends. She told them all about Dan, his kindness, his support for her beliefs and dedication to her faith, and his determination to stay in her life. She also told them that he wasn't Catholic, and there was a big difference in how much money they made; as a computer whiz for investment firms, she made several times what he did, even in his new job as ground crew personnel at the airport. "I could have said 'Oh, he doesn't make enough money,' but I didn't. You have to be open to it and confident enough in yourself. He's not corporate this or that, but that doesn't matter. I could marry some big corporate CEO and never see him, but I'd have a pretty diamond ring. . . . That's not what it's about."

The question of faith was more difficult for Michele. "We were up all night talking," Michele said. "And my girlfriends finally told me that Dan had to be in love with me and I was crazy not to see it. I denied it, but the next day I called him and told him what they had said.

"He was like, 'What? Don't you know that?' But I didn't know whether he loved me because he hadn't said the words. I got all embarrassed and we changed the topic."

As Dan was leaving after his next visit to Seattle, he told Michele he loved her. "I couldn't speak. I couldn't get the words out and I was turning red as I tried to mumble and choke out something. I was just overwhelmed. I loved him so much, but I was frustrated with our situation and didn't know what it was going to mean for us in the future."

Over the next few weeks, the emails flew back and forth more rapidly. The distance was getting to be too much for them, and one afternoon, the big status-of-the-relationship conversation led to confessions of frustration about all the obstacles between them. The last part of the exchange read:

<Michele> writes

This is so frustrating! Let's just run off to Italy and get married!!

<Dan> writes

OK.

"I freaked out. I had just asked him to marry me without even realizing it and he'd said yes!" Michele said. "I wrote back and said call me, call me right now! We talked for two hours and we were engaged. It was incredible." Two months later, Dan and Michele were married at the courthouse in Denver with only their closest family and friends in attendance. They then left for a honeymoon in New York City.

The reaction within the church was much more welcoming than Michele had expected. "I met with a priest in my church and told him about Dan, and that we were getting married. He was really supportive. He said I had made my choice and now I needed to be faithful and loyal to my husband," Michele remembered. "I had been a Catholic on my own for 35 years and I wasn't going to give that up. I didn't want Dan to convert. That wasn't the point. I was in love with him and who he was. He swore that if I stopped practicing my religion, I wouldn't be the same person either. He's so supportive.

"I'm a firm believer that everything that happened to me can happen to others. I was 35 when I got married, so that should be good news to everyone."

Always a bridesmaid?

There are two waves of marriages. The first is a boom in the mid-20s, when it seems as if the whole world is getting married except you. Many high-achieving women begin to panic at this stage because they aren't a part of it. The second big wave of marriages takes place in the early to mid-30s. That's when it's more likely for those among the SWANS to glide to the altar.

The First Wave

Raquel, a 25-year-old who works at a private equity firm, has been receiving thick calligraphied envelopes at an increasingly rapid rate. She's in the midst of the first wave. "All my friends are getting engaged and now I'm starting to worry," she said. "OK, not worry, really, but be aware of it. All of them are successful and smart. I'm really happy for them. But while I don't feel old, when I turned 25 I said, how did I get that old? I just don't want to grow up. I don't have a five-year plan."

According to the original Harris Interactive data collected for this book, one-third of SWANS are concerned that they are going to be "left behind" as all their other friends marry. And indeed, different life stages can mean trouble for friendships. Eighty-four percent of women and 78 percent of men said they have lost or become estranged from friends because they were in different phases of their lives.

In the first wave of weddings, SWANS need to brace themselves: You're going to be a bridesmaid or a solo guest a lot. You won't get that plus-one option very often, and you'll suffer through yet another *rendition of "I Will Survive" on the dance floor with the rest of the single girls. I attended seven weddings in one year and went solo to every single one. At one, I was the only unmarried bridesmaid, so the makeup artist did her best to turn me into the sexy seductress of the bunch.*

Make an effort at these weddings—you never know who you might meet. Check out what you like and don't like about each of the events so you'll be prepared for your own. And be thrilled for your friends. They're going to be excited to dance at your big day soon.

The Second Wave

The second wave hits in the early 30s. This is the time when the majority of SWANS walk down the aisle. By age 34, 79 percent of women with advanced degrees and 81 percent of high-earning women have married. By age 39 those numbers spike to 88 percent and 84 percent, respectively.

Still no steady boyfriend as this round gets started? Cynthia, a 34-year-old married high-achiever, said she hears the worry in her single friends' voices during the second wave. "The anxiety creeps in around the early 30s. I just try to be a good friend—and I keep saying 'Someday your prince will come,'" she said.

There's no need to panic. The early 30s are just the beginning of the nuptials for SWANS, and your turn is coming soon. Ask the groom to sit you next to his eligible friend at the reception. And perhaps request that the bride eschew the bouquet toss.

The Third Wave?

For Amy, 42, it was a good idea to wait out both these waves. "I think in some ways I decided not to get married until I was a hundred percent sure. So it may serve me well in the future because I think I know a lot more about myself now," she said. "What I've found is dating at 42 is so much different than dating in your twenties.

"I was 25 or 24 and my mother said, 'Now you need to meet your future husband at business school. Your sister did. This is your chance,'" remembered Amy. "I felt a lot of pressure to go to a high-powered business school and to find a husband. It was over-whelming. The one guy that I developed a crush on was also a late bloomer and is just getting married at 42. I just talked to him the other day. He's finally getting married. It's kind of fun because there are a number of late bloomers from my business school class, mostly men. There are some good possibilities out there still!"

Chapter 7

The Clock Is on the Field?

If I stay on this merry-go-round, she thought, I'm going to become very accomplished, just the sort of girl no man will ever marry.

—JAMES BALDWIN, "COME OUT
THE WILDERNESS" (1965)

ON A SUMMER EVENING three friends met for drinks in New York City. Vera, 27, is poised and well spoken. She has a law degree and a master's in international affairs and works for a poverty research council. Since graduate school, she's been dating Grant, who currently works in Louisiana as an entrepreneur. To take the next step in the relationship means sacrificing one of their careers so that they can live in the same place, and Vera isn't sure she can take that step just yet.

Jennifer, 28, a lanky, well-spoken blond, recently finished her master's in public affairs and now works at an international aid organization. She's dating a younger guy who has just moved to Washington, DC, and though she's pretty sure he's the one, she's frustrated that the relationship isn't progressing as fast as she'd like.

Sarah, 27, is energetic and passionate about politics. She's worked on several campaigns and now has a permanent role organizing events for a New York politician. She's single and frustrated that her work schedule is so unreliable. She cancels on her friends and dates all the time because of work. But she's feeling the maternal pull—and she wants to settle down. She's just not sure where love will fit into her busy schedule.

Vera: *In my law school program, everyone was very young and it was a dating atmosphere, not a settling down vibe. It was a big deal if someone got engaged. But at [the international affairs school], people were going insane about marriage. So I freaked out. Everyone was getting married.*

Now, I don't know what the next step should be. I've worked very hard to build a life that was comfortable and safe here, and I'm finding the idea of giving that up to be very disconcerting. Grant is so supportive, he's fine. I'm having an internal struggle. Career or man?

It's OK to say I want to be a wife and a mother, but not yet. I want to marry Grant. If he asked me, I'd say yes, but there's no way in hell he's going to ask me now, and that wouldn't be my ideal either. My ideal would be to rewind to age 24 and to be ready in three years. I'm not ready now, but I know I should be.

Jennifer: *I've been purposefully dating since college. But in the last few years I've felt the anxiety. And now it's this big thing. It's always present. I'm at a stage in the relationship—it's been a year and eight months—and I know the exact date. I would say yes if he asked.*

My parents always said I had plenty of time, but in the last few months they've been asking questions and making comments. They both call me and say it's not a good idea to continue dating him. "You have to have a serious talk with him about his intentions," my dad said. Mom says I should give him until October and then pull the plug.

This has already put a wedge between me and my family. I know it's because they love me and want me to be happy and they are concerned he's not as serious. The whole extended family is talking about this.

Sarah: *I can't handle that I'm a project that people have to worry about. I've said to my family "I don't want you talking about this—I don't need 'working out.'"*

My mom shifted in the last two years. She always said if I wanted to be a lawyer or a doctor, boys weren't to distract me. But now she's started asking about grandchildren, saying I shouldn't work so hard and "When are you going to meet someone?"

Jennifer: *I'm still working out some of my own anxieties and this isn't helping, but I don't want my parents to be making that breaking point [come] even faster. They push you to defend the opposite position.*

I've never felt this way about anyone before. My parents said that I could go out and search for a husband and find someone who meets the right criteria. I could do that. But I want more. I feel so strongly [that] it's worth waiting to see how this relationship works out.

It's all about timing for Vera, Jennifer, and Sarah. They know successful women like themselves will marry later than other women, but how much later? And where do you meet guys when you work 80 hours a week and are too exhausted to go out on a Saturday night? Parents are putting on the pressure for wedding bells and grandchildren. Somehow, marriage has become another item on the to-do list, and these women, like many SWANS, worry that the clock is going to run out.

In the past 35 years, American men and women have been marrying at increasingly older ages. According to U.S. Census data, in 1970, only 19 percent of women *hadn't* walked down the aisle by the end of their 20s. Today, some 40 percent of women are single on their 30th birthday. And for high-achievers, this trend is even more pronounced. The average woman with a graduate degree marries for the first time near the age of 30, according to the U.S. Census, but the national median age of marriage for women hovers around 25. So in that initial wave of late-20s weddings, high-achieving women may be feeling a little panic: Friends are walking down the aisle as SWANS wait for their turn.

About 90 percent of women in the United States marry by the age of 44. High-achieving women are just as likely to marry as their less successful sisters—they just do so a little later. According to the 2005 Current Population Survey, the most reliable and recent national data available, 55 percent of women with graduate degrees have married in the 25–29 age bracket compared with 61 percent of women without graduate degrees. But that gap closes rapidly: Among women ages 30 to 34, 79 percent with advanced degrees *and* with less education have married. And among women ages 35 to 39, those with graduate degrees seem slightly more likely to have walked down the aisle: 88 percent of women with advanced degrees, compared with 86 percent of women with a college degree or less have been married.

The same patterns are true for women who are high-earners: Among women ages 25 to 29, 58 percent in the top 10 percent of earners for their age group have married, compared with 61 percent of other women. But by the 30–34 age bracket, high-earners have pulled ahead slightly: 81 percent of high-earning women have walked down the aisle, compared to 79 percent of all other women.

Even among the uber-high-earners—those women earning between $100,000 and $250,000 per year—the data hold true. Cities versus suburbs? Yes, it's still true: High-achieving women are marrying at the same rates nationwide. In fact, among women ages 30 to 44 who live in a major urban center—a city with a population of 1 million or more—a larger percentage of women who earn $100,000 per year have married than their lower-earning sisters. Eighty-eight percent of these high-achieving women have married compared to 82 percent of other women.

Yes, there's a lot of good news for high-achieving women—but the fact remains that successful women stay single longer. Why? It takes time, energy, and devotion to build a career, so many of these women are focusing on their professional lives in their 20s and looking toward the future a bit later. Plus, there has been a major culture shift in terms of expectations for women: Today it is a real option for smart, strong women to stay single until they find the right person. In fact, my new data finds that 81 percent of high-achieving women report they aren't focused on getting married—they are living their lives to the fullest right now.

"Successful woman have a choice—they don't have to get married out of desperation," feminist writer Katha Pollit said in an interview. "Fifty years ago you'd probably be married to a guy who doesn't make you happy. Aren't you happier on your own?" Yes, but timing is everything, and for SWANS who feel they are ready to commit, there is pressure from parents, friends—and, often most keenly felt, the pressure they put on themselves—to find Mr. Right.

Timing

Building a career takes time, effort, and dedication. A young woman's investment in her education—working hard to earn top grades in college, applying to and excelling at graduate school, passing all the necessary board certifications and tests—is an investment in her social capital: the skills that make her a good job candidate for the future. But all these take hard work. And then there's the long climb to the top of whatever field she chooses.

My new survey data demonstrate that high-achieving single women are prioritizing their careers and educations in their 20s and early 30s. Some 60 percent of high-achieving single women ages 25 to 34 said that their educational or career success was their top priority at this point in their lives, compared with 42 percent of single 35- to 40-year-old women.

One SWANS said she made a vow not to date in business school, for fear that she would get distracted. Another SWANS spends 16-hour days working on her research. "I do go out a bit, but I don't have time to coordinate my schedule with someone else," she said.

For Jody, a 31-year-old neuroscience researcher, there was the PhD, and now the postdoctoral fellowship. She works 14-hour days in her lab and said time is going by so fast. "I worry about being left out, left behind. My friends are getting married and having babies. But do I feel like I'm missing out? I don't know . . . I think I'm having more fun," she said. "I want a life partner and I'm wondering if the pool of available guys is diminishing. But this isn't a business transaction, and I try not to think of it that way." Most of the women she works with are married with children. "I haven't interacted with single female academicians, so I've always thought I can do both."

Though Jody doesn't believe that it's her education or her career that's holding her back, she is worried about how the timing will come together. She has a crush on a fellow researcher in Boston, but the two meet only at academic conferences. "We're both at intermediate stages in our career. We're both looking for high-level faculty positions at prestigious institutions, and it's difficult to coordinate that kind of ambition in a couple," she said. "I am holding out hope, because I'm not interested in other people." In the next four years, Jody expects she'll move several times as other research positions become available. "I'm not looking forward to moving around, but I know it will be at least five years until I'm settled."

Medical doctors also have a costly investment in their careers throughout their 20s. Even for women who head to medical school straight after college, four years of school training plus another four years of residency means a heavy workload and inflexible schedule until nearly age 30. "You can't start a relationship in residency. Everyone tells you that," said Shayna, a young doctor beginning her residency in New York. "It's scary, because if I go in alone, I'll be alone for the next four years," worried her friend Nadia.

Anne, a doctor in Boston, said concerns like that are all too common. She never thought she would be single at age 30. "I've been ready to be married since my mid-20s. I would choose family if I had to choose between my career and family." After medical school, Anne took an extra year to figure out whether she wanted to continue on for her residency. With the grueling hours of medical training, she knew her "whole life would be put on hold." She's finishing up her residency now and hoping to meet someone soon. "I believe I can do both: career and family. It's going to be different than it would have been if I'd met someone 10 years ago, but it can work," she said. "I might be better off meeting someone at 32. I've taken on my own challenges."

Finding the time to meet men, and to keep a relationship alive, is challenging in those early stages of a successful business career. Raquel, 25, said she works 10- to 18-hour days at her private equity firm. "It's hard to plan ahead and commit. I cancel a lot." She said she dates as much as she can, given the long hours her job demands, and she's not worried. "What gives me hope is to see the number of people who meet in their 30s and are so happy. It's the person who you're going to spend the rest of your life with—you can wait a few years."

Patricia, a 32-year-old Washington attorney, wants to make partner, and she doesn't feel she has time for dating. "I work seven days a week and am often in the office until 10 p.m. It's hard to go out on weekday evenings." Many of her male colleagues have a wife at home. "I wish I had someone to take care of my personal life," she said ruefully.

Patricia's complaint is a common one: She's looking for a supportive man who will help her on her path to becoming partner. Kama, a consultant in Chicago, echoes Patricia's thoughts. She believes that if she had married her college boyfriend, she would never have gone to business school and never landed this fantastic job she loves. But she's wondering where and how she'll meet the kind of man she's looking for. "I'm not a bitter person, but I do get into this funk every few weeks and I wonder if there is no one out there for me, to just chill and open a bottle of wine and watch TV . . . to support me."

According to my new data, 76 percent of SWANS and 74 percent of single men said they found it hard to meet people they would be interested in dating or having a relationship with. But it's not that these singles feel they are too busy: 57 percent of SWANS disagreed with the statement "I don't have enough time for my personal life." Rather, it's a constant balance.

"Guys want you to be available when they want you to be available," said Hope, 30, and building her marketing career makes it challenging to always be around for dates. Kama agreed: She said the travel schedule of her job makes it difficult to establish a new relationship. "Men need to know you're going to make time for them. If I'm traveling all the time, I just can't do it."

"I work until eight or nine p.m. and then I'm on the computer working when I get home," said Hope. "The workload is a lot—but it's also my nature to get things done and I'm a perfectionist." Amid the career push, Hope said she wonders where she's going to meet the man of her dreams. "I'm not going to meet him on my walk from the office to the car," she said, laughing.

Kama said she meets a lot of people on airplanes during her business travels. But after a long week of traveling and late nights, she often stays home instead of going out to try to meet men. "It's my choice—I choose not to go on a lot of Friday nights out and meet people. And I've moved around a lot. I chose to move. I chose to focus on my career. I chose to not go on dates with guys who don't meet my specifications."

New York matchmaker Nancy Slotnick said she worries about women like this. If marriage is a priority, she advises smart, success-ful women to be willing and ready to put in time and effort for the search. According to her program, a woman must invest 15 hours each week in the search for a man. Most of her clients initially balk at this. "Why is that so much? To run a marathon, or to look for a job takes that long. Why not your love life?" Slotnick asked. She tells women that they can have the career, the husband, and the family, but it takes work. "If you aren't taking serious action with your personal life you are inadvertently putting it off. High-achieving women shouldn't be afraid or embarrassed to use their skills to get the man they want," she said. " 'I'm really busy' *isn't* an excuse."

One of the benefits for older SWANS is that they are at a higher level in their careers, or perhaps even run their own business, and can devote this level of time and energy to their personal lives, said Amy, 42. "Before, I had to . . . pay my dues and work quite a bit harder, whereas now I've kind of earned the reward and I can work remotely and I can take days off here and there and I really have a great schedule. I think it would be easier [to meet someone] now, and I'm lucky because I'm in a business where you are running your own business within a business and you can . . . do what you want."

Amy would advise women who want to marry and have children earlier to make time for dating in their 20s through careful planning and forethought. "I would say to . . . map out what your goals are and to choose a profession that would allow you to juggle a personal life."

Christina

On a January afternoon, Christina drove to an offsite meeting with a more senior public affairs officer at her company. The two women were talking about the upcoming meeting when she asked Christina if she'd seen Maureen Dowd's column in the *New York Times* that day. "Don't ever get married," said the older woman, reaching into the backseat to grab the paper and handing it to Christina. "See?"

Christina read the column. "A few years ago at a White House Correspondents' dinner, I met a very beautiful actress. Within moments, she blurted out: 'I can't believe I'm 46 and not married. Men only want to marry their personal assistants or P.R. women,'" wrote Dowd.[1] Christina kept reading: "I'd been noticing a trend along these lines, as famous and powerful men took up with the young women whose job it was to tend to them and care for them in some way: their secretaries, assistants, nannies, caterers, flight attendants, researchers and fact-checkers. . . . Women want to be in a relationship with guys they can seriously talk to—unfortunately, a lot of those guys want to be in relationships with women they don't have to talk to."

With her colleague egging her on, Christina said, the two of them laughed somewhat bitterly about the truth of the article. But during her meeting, Christina's mind wandered back to the column, and to her boyfriend. Was it really true? Was she, as a successful, intelligent woman, never going to get married?

About a year earlier, Christina, then 34, had decided she needed to branch out. She'd had enough experiences with the club girls, the investment bankers, and the southern football players. She wanted to meet someone "outside my set." She had started a different job and wasn't quite entrenched. She had some time, and she posted a profile on TheOnion.com.

Choosing a screen name was difficult; all the ones she considered were already taken. Frustrated by the online dating process, she entered "aggravating" as her screen name. She chose to list herself as interested in "friendship and dating" rather than "a serious relationship" and listed "lip balm" and "irony" as the things she couldn't live without. "I just wanted to meet some new people," Christina said.

"I went out with three guys and had fun, but I was getting so distracted by weeding out the messages from these guys. You've got your picture up there, and you see all of these guys with their pictures. They email, you say 'Eh,' and then you go back and forth and you try to decide if you want to meet this guy. It was getting a bit much. So I decided I was going to take my profile down and just be done with it.

"But then I got this message from this guy," she said, smiling. "It was a corny email. He said somebody told him that Scorpios and Capricorns were a good match. I'm a Scorpio, he's a Capricorn." Christina checked out his profile; he looked cute and was from the South. "I'm from North Carolina, you know, so I was like, 'I'm going to meet him. But this is it. No more online dating after this.'"

That was Josh.

Christina and Josh took it slow in the beginning, she said. "He courted me and we kind of courted each other, and the whole time I was thinking, 'OK, I'm taking a different approach to dating. I'm not going to worry about if he likes me. I'm going to worry about whether or not I like him.' "

A few weeks into their relationship, Christina and Josh had "a miscommunication": a "weird kind of thing in the beginning," she called it. "I called him up and I'm like, 'I don't know what happened but let's figure this out.' And we decided early, you know, let's talk to each other and not be jerks. We had a nice long getting-to-know-you stage and then we fell in love with each other and, well, here we are."

Yes, Josh was from the South, but he wasn't like the men Christina had dated before. Josh was a documentary producer, he didn't own a suit, and, unlike her, he didn't know much about mortgages and markets. She was a businesswoman and, he, "well, he's kind of an artist," she said. "I tell him about my office politics and he likes to hear those stories, but he doesn't really want to live it."

She thought again about the Maureen Dowd column: Was Josh put off by her career or her ambition? "Josh would never be intimidated by success," she said. "He's extremely driven himself. The film he's working on now is his make-or-break film, he considers. He's got a major distributor and he's like, 'This is it.' And he wants to be successful, but the success of his career and the success of my career are a little different," she mused. No, she thought, he wasn't intimidated by her income or her job. Things were really pretty good. The two were equally matched in terms of professional success, and when his career in production took off, he might even be outearning her.

Still, her conversation with her work colleague and the depressing conclusion of the Maureen Dowd article gnawed at her. "That was Thursday," remembered Christina. "And the following Monday I got engaged. The timing was impeccable."

Balancing Choices

"We don't have to get married. Our mother's generation had to get married. For my mother, there were educational opportunities she couldn't pursue, but she still got a master's, and yet there was more she wanted to do," said Julia, 37, a lawyer who recently married. "Now there are a lot fewer have-tos. I've thought about having fewer choices and how it would be easier. It's a bit overwhelming, all the things we can do, but at our core, we like it that way."

SWANS talk a lot about "life balance": how to work hard, play hard, and find time for relaxation along the way. One married high-achieving woman was so busy that her husband accompanied her to get a pedicure so he could spend time with her. "He even had his nails painted dark purple," she said. Two other SWANS said they were taking up art classes to add balance to their lives. But few said that they had it all figured out.

"In the last couple years I've made very proactive attempts to do better about it," said Rebecca, 32. For several years she had been commuting more than an hour to work, and she recently changed jobs to reduce her commute. "I can see my friends more after work sometimes and do more social things. I don't think that it's a perfect balance, but I make it work," she said.

Madeline, 31, describes herself as "a driven workaholic" who recently realized the benefits of a balanced life. "I'm getting out there and meeting people. You have to make a conscious effort to get out there, with the mind-set of being enthusiastic."

Questions about balance and timing for the future hit a nerve with SWANS nationwide. At a book club meeting in New York, Kim, Angela, Star, and Jill worried about how the decisions they made now might affect their futures.

Star, 25, is currently living with her boyfriend but worried that his new job might force him to leave the city. And then what was the right step for her? "Right now I'm doing this job and this relationship, and in a year I could be totally different. I don't want to move to follow him. By being married, it could stop our dreams. Maybe once I'm older I can settle down," she said.

"It all comes down to timing," her friend Kim, 29, agreed. "I see myself being 32 when I get married, but that's two years away, so maybe 33. The scary age for me is 37. It used to be 35, but I've pushed it up.

"When I was a summer associate, a single junior associate said that I needed to be in a relationship before I started at the firm, because once you start, you'll never meet anyone," continued Kim. "You don't want to date your coworkers, and it's hard to break out of the office."

"Older single women put out a vibe that they are desperate to get married. Don't do that!" admonished Star. "Don't push it. I met my boyfriend online."

Jill, 28, said the most important lesson she learned about timing was when to call it quits. She stayed in a relationship for five years before she realized it wasn't going to work out. "I'd encourage women not to be afraid to leave a relationship. Don't stay too long. If it's not working, leave. No one says 'I got out of that relationship too early'—they regret how much time they spent in a dead-end partnership." And, she continued, a major part of creating the right timing for a relationship is attitude: "Be happy with your life. People notice if someone is lonely. You should have your own thing going on. I have a friend who has just accepted the fact that she might not ever meet anyone, and she's fine with that. I bet she's going to get married next year."

Kim sighed. "I feel like the older we get, the more we do a mental somersault that the alternative is OK. At some point friends all say they are comfortable with being single. You mentally prepare yourself. I still think I'll get married, but I'm not sure what that's based on."

Michele

Four dogs tugged at their leashes and Michele and Dan broke into a run in Central Park one recent summer afternoon in New York City. To celebrate their fifth anniversary, Michele, 40, and Dan, 38, were spending the day together in the park and going out for a nice dinner. The couple had discussed going away for a romantic trip, but Dan's new furry clients were keeping him busy.

Michele and Dan moved to New York from Denver a few years after they married because Michele landed a job at a top investing and advisory group. Her salary increased dramatically, and soon she was making four times what Dan earned as a ground crew attendant at a national airline.

The couple enjoyed living in New York City, but Dan was antsy for fresh air and exercise. So when he was laid off during major cutbacks at his airline, Dan and Michele brainstormed about a new career for him: dog walking. "He loved animals, so we said, let's see if we can make this happen," Michele said. With her business savvy, Michele drew up a business plan, determined rates, and made business cards. She organized publicity and insurance, and Dan built his client base.

In the beginning, he had only a few dogs to walk in the neighborhood. He'd pick them up, walk them to the park, and bring them home. But once word got around that he was reliable, business began to increase. After a year and a half, Dan had 30 dogs and two employees—and his business had turned into a small company producing serious income.

For their fifth anniversary, Michele took the day off from work in the financial services world and walked dogs with Dan. "That's the coolest thing about being married and being together. I'm thrilled he can do this. He inspires me," Michele said.

"It's really a partnership. And Michele is the business mind behind it," Dan said approvingly.

"Marriage is not a pissing contest," Dan continued. "It's not about money or who is more successful. It's about two people who love to be together, and anything that's good that happens to one should make the other happy."

Michele credits some of Dan's ideas to his mother, who worked hard and owned and expanded her own dry-cleaning business. "The fact that his mother wasn't always going to be home making him lunch until he was 25 really shaped him. He always dated very, very successful women. He dated a graphic artist, a pilot. He's never been intimidated and he's just comfortable in his own skin. He's got no misconceptions that a wife needs to be this, this, and this. And that was really attractive."

Dan said he often hears that successful women aren't going to get married, but he doesn't really buy into that idea. "Success has nothing to do with it. Job and status never mattered to me. She makes ten times more than I do and she's smart and good at what she does. Whether Michele wants to continue to climb the ladder or quit and teach French for a tenth of what she currently earns, it's fine with me. The money is a bonus, but if you are genuinely attracted to someone, like I was to Michele, you don't care what she does."

As partners in business and partners in life, Michele and Dan take care of each other. "Before I was married I was the most responsible person in the world. I was never late, I never lost anything. And now that I'm married I'm always late, I lose my keys on a consistent basis, if we're traveling I'm the last one to pack," said Michele.

Looking back, Michele said the timing couldn't have been more perfect for her and Dan. "A lot of people just get married because they wonder 'What if someone else doesn't come along?' So what? If I hadn't met Dan, I'd probably still be single and I'd be perfectly happy. I've been happy 98 percent of my life and I was waiting to meet the love of my life that blows me away." Dan said it was better that he'd had a few years to mature before he met Michele. "Guys get married when they are older, smarter, and maybe more competent and have more experience. And I'm really happy with my wife. Either way, the money thing doesn't bother me."

Michele had watched "a light flash on" in the minds of her single friends as they approached 30. Suddenly they wanted to get married. "My guy friends would describe these women who were desperate to get married and how embarrassing that was. I never wanted to do that. If you are happy with yourself, your environment, the people you surround yourself with, and whatever makes you who you are, and if you can say the majority of your life you are happy, then you are a success and everything else falls into place.

"What's worse: Waking up lonely two mornings out of a year when you don't have anyone to cuddle with, or waking up 365 days miserable? Which would you rather have? I'll take my two days, thank you. This guy had to blow me away."

For Jennifer, Vera, and Sarah the conversation continues. Mixed in with their questions about timing and careers is the question of babies. As she watches her friends from high school have babies, Sarah, the 27-year-old political consultant, wonders if she'll be left behind. Jennifer said she's concerned, too. And Vera wants to make children a priority—but not quite yet.

Sarah: My closest friends are having babies. I'm having pangs. If I'm single at 40, I'm adopting. It used to be 35, but *about two years ago I realized that there were these fantastic 35-, 36-, 38-year-old women who are still cool [laughing].*

Jennifer: *I've been having baby pangs lately, too. But I'd never tell my family that, and I feel like I can't even hold my godchild without the family giving me looks. I would like to have kids, but I'm not at a great place. Ideally in the next three or four years, but I don't know if that's going to happen.*

Vera: *No baby pangs here. I like the idea of kids, but I'm not at all interested in having kids any time soon. No pressure there. Babies aren't that fascinating. I'm scared about having something that is utterly dependent on me. I'm ambitious and mildly resentful at the idea of changing or quitting my job—and I'm lucky that I can do that with kids at home. There's a particular way I want to raise my kids—I want to make them a priority—and I'm not there yet. My mom and dad had me when they were ready for that.*

Sarah: *Yeah, and my family is asking, "When are you going to quit your job and have a kid of your own?" My mom had me when she was my age. She's wondering what's going on with me.*

Am I too old to get married?

There's an old saying that women should "use what Mother Nature gave you before Father Time takes it away." Meaning that a young woman should maximize her beauty to find a man, then marry and have children before her looks diminish and her biological clock stops ticking.

Age is a big issue for high-achieving women in their mid-30s and above. "The media is always showing young and beautiful women—so the message I feel like I get a lot is that I'll get married if I am young and beautiful, or at least cosmetically enhanced. But as an older woman, all natural, the media doesn't make it sound good," said Alexis, a 35-year-old lawyer in San Francisco. "I feel like I have plenty of time, but I'm concerned that men are ruling me out because of my age."

Lindsay, 38, a professor in Boston, looks a decade younger than she is—and said she feels like a girl in her late 20s rather than a woman approaching 40. "I realized a year or two ago when I finished my degree that I was finally getting settled in myself," she said. "I never went out searching for a husband—but just recently it hit me that, wow, I'm old. I'm going to my friends' kids' bar mitzvahs. I missed the marriage round and now we're already on the bar mitzvah round and I'm not even out of the gate? I still think of myself as 28," she said.

Alexis and Lindsay ask themselves: Am I too old to find a man?

Americans are marrying later overall, so a woman in her 30s is more likely to have never married. According to census data, some 24 percent of American women ages 30 to 34 and 15 percent of women ages 35 to 39 have never married. But the trend is even more pronounced for men. Thirty-two percent of men ages 30 to 34 and 23 percent of men ages 35 to 39 have never married.[2]

These later marriage rates are helpful for SWANS: If all Americans are marrying later, then the time a high-achieving woman spends investing in her education and career in her early and mid-20s isn't nearly as "costly" in the marriage market.

You're never too old to find love. In fact, as a successful woman, age is even less of an obstacle. New national data show that never-married successful women in their 30s are more likely to walk down the aisle than their less-accomplished age-mates. There's a 66 percent chance that a 30-year-old woman will marry if she has a college degree or less, but there's a 75 percent chance she'll be a bride if she has an advanced degree.

Later marriage has its benefits. Increased education, maturity, and stability make for happier marriages. Research suggests that successful marriages are more likely to occur when both members of the couple are mature and "ready" and when the couple has a secure financial status. Both of these characteristics are likely to increase with age.

But like the defeatist notion that SWANS are overqualified for love, it's a self-fulfilling prophecy to say you're too old to meet and marry a great man. Make an effort to look and feel your best at any age. Pamper yourself into believing you are beautiful (a manicure-pedicure and a free makeover at the cosmetics counter always does wonders for me). Then go out and make it happen.

Be open to older and younger men. If you are only as old as you feel, so is he—don't be too quick to judge. Go to events and parties that target the proper age and type of person you want to meet. Hanging out at a dive bar during spring break isn't going to yield a whole lot of eligible 40-year-old men, but a business networking event, a charity fund-raiser, an art exhibition, or a rock-climbing class might give you better results.

The desire for children is NOT a reason to settle for a man you don't love or to rush—and ruin—a relationship with a man you care about. Pay attention to your biological clock. We've made a lot of advancements, but Mother Nature and Father Time are still strict taskmasters. But also recognize that adoption is a viable and wonderful option.

With age comes experience and self-awareness. Take it from Adrianna, 42, a dentist in Tucson: "Singleness is uniqueness to me. Now I'm ready to share that. I know who I am and what I want."

Chapter 8

Shattering the Myth of the Baby Bust

THE MYTH OF THE BARREN female executive holds that women delay marriage and childbirth to suit their career needs, and then suddenly realize it's too late to make babies. This theory was most prominently espoused by Sylvia Ann Hewlett in *Creating a Life,* her 2001 book about high-achieving women. Hewlett reported that almost half of all professional women are childless at age 40—and for the most part, it wasn't a choice.

Hewlett argued that successful women were faced with a "creeping non-choice": After delaying having children for years as they built their careers, they find they have waited too long. They are no longer fertile and realize that the choice not to have children was made without their ever even realizing they were making it.

The myth of the barren female executive is based on the assumption that women can be mothers, or they can have successful careers, but not both. This myth comes from the idea that women who work outside the home can't be as good or loving mothers as the women who stay home full-time. Of all the myths that hold successful women back as they strive for excellence in their careers and happiness in their personal lives, this one may be the most damaging.

And yet the media, and many successful young women, believe these dire findings to be universally true for all ambitious women. Why? Because unfortunately, for many previous generations, it was true.

According to research by Harvard professor Claudia Goldin, among women who were born between 1944 and 1957 (women who would be 50 to 63 years old in 2007) who graduated from college and worked full-time, nearly 50 percent were childless by ages 37 to 47.[1]

Even as recently as the 1980 Census, women with professional or doctoral qualifications were twice as likely to have no children at home at age 40 compared with women with a high school degree and some college.[2] And more generally, Elaina Rose, a professor at the University of Washington, finds that in 1980 a woman with a professional or doctoral degree was 18.2 percent less likely to be a mother than a woman with a bachelor's degree.[3]

But Professor Rose has also found some very good news for young SWANS and successful married women: Things are improving. In each subsequent census, married women were increasingly likely to have children and a career. By 2010, she hopes—and predicts—that the success penalty will have disappeared. "The perception that women face a stark choice between career and marriage is incorrect," she said. "Young women no longer need to feel pressure to limit investments in their careers in order to enhance their opportunities in terms of marriage, and perhaps motherhood."[4]

Already there are many signs of this good news. According to the 2001 Current Population Survey research, 78 percent of married high-achieving women ages 36 to 40 have kids. That's *exactly* the same number as all other married women who work full-time.[5] Studies of elite women reflect similar patterns: A study of 187 women attending a recent *Fortune* Magazine Most Powerful Women in Business Summit found that a full 71 percent were mothers, and an earlier Catalyst report found that 64 percent of female vice presidents and top leaders in Fortune 1,000 companies have children, and more than 72 percent are married.[6]

The reality is that high-achieving women want to get married and have children—and most do just that. The untold story is a story of marriage: High-achieving women are less likely than other women to have children outside of marriage. Birth rates for college-educated unmarried women are substantially below the rates for less-educated unmarried women, the National Center for Health Statistics found. Among unmarried mothers age 25 and older, only 9 percent had college degrees.[7] But when you compare high-achieving married women to their married peers, the baby gap disappears.

Indeed, the negative perceptions of a successful woman's maternal qualities are slowly fading as well. In the new national research for this book, more than 1,600 high-achieving men and women were asked if they agreed or disagreed with the statement "Mothers of young children should not work outside the home." Only 20 percent of women and 35 percent of men agreed.

The vast majority of high-achieving women report that having a family is an important aspect of their future dreams, and 75 percent of women without children say they would like to have children in the future. Indeed, one single college professor in Boston said she believed she was "put on this earth to be a mother and have a family."

But most high-achieving women do not feel pressure to have children until they are ready, which may be well into their 30s. "I want children, but I'm in no rush," said Zoe, 29, a lawyer in Washington, DC. "I wonder if I'll continue to work as hard as I do now. I have ideas, but I don't have anything set in stone. Right now, it's not the right time, and my husband is totally understanding, although he wants kids a bit sooner." Kathleen, 27, from Oklahoma, said she and her fiancé have had similar conversations. "We won't have kids for a while. We'll wait until I'm 33 or so, but we go back and forth on that. I want to be married for at least two years before kids," she said.

For younger SWANS, having children is a "maybe," an aspect of growing up and being an adult that lies in the future. But that doesn't mean that successful women in their 20s take a cavalier attitude toward their most fertile years. Among high-achieving women ages 25 to 34, 76 percent said they would like to have a child, or have another child. So it's not surprising that nearly every discussion about the future turns into a discussion about the when and how of children.

To Star, 25, a sales executive who is living with her boyfriend, marriage and children go hand in hand. "I want to get married when I want to have kids, and not really anytime sooner. I'm considering freezing my eggs," she said firmly, igniting a debate among her girlfriends.

"I don't want to ever get married to have kids. I want a family, but I don't want the kids to be the driving force," responded Kim, a 29-year-old attorney. "I'm frustrated by the fact that my eggs are dying. I would like to be a wife before being a mother."

Jill agreed, but said she was frustrated by how she has had to put off children to invest in her career. "If you go to grad school, it's just not possible to have kids by 30. I never thought I'd marry young, but I'd love to be married at 30. I don't know if that's going to happen," said the 28-year-old nonprofit executive. "I also want four kids . . . have two of my own, and adopt two? Either way, I've got to get going."

For Angela, 31, the only one of the group who is not in a relationship, the topic of children is a touchy one. "I've accepted that

I might not have children," she said. Angela, a petite brunette with a button nose, said she hasn't dated anyone seriously in more than a year. "I don't like being single and I'd like to get married. I'd like to share my life with someone. But every day you should think about using your talents. God gave them to you, and you need to use them. You don't know what's going to happen tomorrow, so have a goal, but don't make it your focal point."

According to the original research conducted for this book, successful young women don't have reason to panic. In 2005, 73 percent of married high-earning women ages 40 to 44 had children, and 77 percent of married women with advanced degrees had children. In both cases, women who earned less or had less education were not any more likely to have children. Gone are the days when a woman must choose between a family and a fulfilling career: Millions of young women are making the most of their opportunities today.

Still, watching friends and relatives build families can be difficult for successful women who aren't at that stage quite yet. Some 47 percent of high-achieving women who don't have children said they are worried that they won't be able to have children. That includes Rebecca, 32, a divorced SWANS, who said she was "going to forget about" the idea of children for now. "For me it's been a hard question. I don't want to be with someone just to have children with them. I don't want that to at some point become the driver of why I'm in a relationship. But I think the older you get, there are questions like that, and it becomes an issue. It would be a wonderful thing if children were an opportunity I had in my life. But until I meet the right person, I'm not going to worry about it," she said.

Rebecca, who lives in New York City, said every time she turns around she feels like she's dodging a stroller. In her mind, this signals a baby boom in the works. "It's colossal," she said. "I mean, people who haven't noticed there's a baby boom must be sleeping.

Maybe this is what it looked like after World War II . . . everyone's pregnant. And the people who aren't pregnant are getting pregnant or just had a baby."

In Manhattan, the number of children under age 5 increased more than 26 percent between 2000 and 2004.[8] And at 32, this is a constant reminder to Rebecca, who has babies on her mind. "I think it's something that people think about, especially those people who aren't with someone. My fundamental perspective is you should enjoy whatever stage of life you are in because that allows you to take advantage of all the great things that happen at that particular point and also to . . . live that experience fully to be able to be ready to be in a different place."

The Facts on Fertility

A woman's educational level is the best predictor of how many children she will have, according to a National Center for Health Statistics study of birth certificates. The highest birth rates occur among women with the lowest educational attainment. For women with college degrees, the birth rate is 1.7 for non-Hispanic white women, 1.6 for black women, and 2.0 for Hispanic women. For women who have a high school degree or less, the birth rate soars to nearly 3 births per woman.[9]

A woman is in her optimal fertility phase between the ages of 18 and 28. There's a 94 percent chance that a healthy 25- to 29-year-old woman can become pregnant, and a 70 percent chance that a healthy 35- to 39-year-old woman can become pregnant. After 40, fertility decreases dramatically—and by age 45, only 5 percent of women are fertile.[10]

"The average 40-year-old at home making love with her husband isn't going to get pregnant. The average 35-year-old woman will," said Dr. Robert Howe, an infertility specialist at the Reproductive Science Center of New England.

For women in their late 30s and early 40s who want to become pregnant, in vitro fertilization (IVF)—in which a woman's egg is fertilized outside of her body and then reinserted—has become an increasingly common procedure. Yet monetary costs are high, and the odds of success are not: The live birth rate per transfer of embryos averages only 10 to 12 percent. Among 40-year-old women who attempted to conceive via assisted reproductive technology in 2003, 15.5 percent successfully gave birth; among 43-year-old women, that number decreased to 5.3 percent.[11] Still, some 48,000 babies were born as a result of assisted reproductive technology in 2003.[12]

Dr. John Patrick O'Grady, a perinatologist and obstetrics specialist at Mercy Medical Center in Springfield, Massachusetts, said that in his more that 25 years of clinical experience, he has noticed a "major trend toward late childbearing among especially the affluent—the only ones who can usually afford the manipulations and tests and interventions."

Other doctors have noticed similar trends. "Most of my patients are over 35 or 37 and they have normal, healthy births," said Dr. Susan Grant, an OB/GYN in New York City affiliated with Lenox Hill Hospital and St Lukes/Roosevelt Hospital. "If a woman comes into my office and says, 'I'm so old, I'm 38,' I say, 'Are you kidding me? You're a youngster.' I see women in their 40s having babies. In the last week, I've gotten news of two women, one 43 and one 44, having spontaneous pregnancies. That's the exception to the rule, but there's certainly a trend toward older women giving birth."

There are several ways to test a woman's fertility, the most common of which is a simple test of hormones on the third day of her cycle, said Dr. Howe. This test can give doctors an "80 percent accurate measure as to the possibility of fertility." Family history—the fertility of a woman's mother, sisters, and aunts—is another good indication.

A woman who is 42 might have "young" eggs—eggs that look as good as a 37-year-old's. Yet another woman of that age could already be in premenopause. Dr. Grant said it's hard for her to predict what the cutoff age is for any specific patient's fertility. Still, all doctors agree: If having children is a priority, doing so in your 20s or early 30s is much more advisable than waiting until your late 30s or beyond.

With donor eggs—eggs taken from a younger woman, inseminated with sperm, and inserted into the mother-to-be's womb—women can become pregnant throughout their 50s. The media attention given to these older births "makes women think they can have children longer than they can," said Dr. Howe, who cautioned that the bulk of celebrities who brag about getting pregnant well into their 40s are doing so with donor eggs.

Freezing eggs will be the solution for the future, Dr. Grant said, but for now, the technology is too new to rely on. "This is going to be the way to go for women who want to work and be having babies at age 50. It will be possible at some point, but it's not my business to say if that's a good thing for society."

The Ticking Clock

For SWANS who want children, there are many options. Odds are that a successful woman will marry in plenty of time to have a child with her husband—without the need for medical intervention. But for a woman in her mid-30s who is panicked that she won't meet a man in time to have children, the ticking biological clock can be double trouble. "Only you can decide which way you want to play your life, but you can't rush dating," said dating coach Nancy Slotnick. "People want to collapse the dating process into a shortened period because they are on a fast pace to have babies. Men want to be singled out. They want to know that you want to marry *them,* that you love them, not that you want their sperm."

Increasingly, SWANS are taking the mental pressure off themselves by entertaining a liberating option: to have a child on her own. According to my new data, 50 percent of high-achieving women without children said they would consider having a child on their own. "The biology issue makes me mad," said Laura, 29. "I've been thinking that if I haven't found someone by a certain age, I'll ask my ex to donate sperm. I joke about it, but I don't know. I'd consider having kids by myself. I have certainly thought about it," she said.

"If at 35 I'm not with someone, I'll consider the single mom thing," said Anne, a 30-year-old medical resident in Boston. "As a doctor, I'd advise women to think about having kids when they are younger, in their early 20s. But this just isn't practical for high-achieving women. And it's a disconnect that lies in our biological challenge of reproduction." Anne said she's confident she'll meet someone and get married, but she's a little disappointed that it's taken so long. "The downside is that I really wanted that special time for just the two of us, before kids and family, and I'm not sure I'll have that."

Some SWANS call it "the dreaded 35": the infamous tipping-point age when a woman is tagged as of "advanced maternal age" if she hasn't already had a child. "I hope those studies about eggs going bad after 35 aren't true. I know we need to get rolling, but honestly, I'm not in a rush," said Cynthia, 35, who has been married for several years.

When the 35 mark has come and gone and they haven't met the right man, more and more SWANS are taking matters into their own hands. "I'm on the verge of a change. I'm trying to have a baby on my own," said Marcia, a 41-year-old San Francisco business executive, smiling confidently. "I've always wanted to get married and have kids. When I was about to turn 40, the window was closing. It seemed very freeing to uncouple the two decisions. At what point do you get on with your life?"

Marcia said she hasn't been dating much as she's been trying to conceive, but she is hopeful that if she has a child, it won't hurt her dating prospects, and she believes it is "pretty likely" that she'll get married. "I would be interested in a man who is interested in children—so what would he have against a baby or toddler that didn't have a father?" Marcia points to Hollywood as a leading indicator: "Actresses aren't waiting to have kids and they are doing it on their own," she said. So now that she has earned enough money to support herself, her child, and a nanny, Marcia is excited about the possibility of being a mother.

When she told her close friends and family, everyone was very supportive. "I told people initially because I wanted to get a sense of what it would be like for the kid—and everyone was very accepting. My parents would have preferred a more conventional route, but they are OK with it," she said. "I remember feeling happy, relieved, and free that I could choose to have this. This is a choice I can make on my own, and that's really freeing."

For Carolyn, 36, a single small-business owner in New Jersey, her fear that her "eggs are dying—packing up and walking out, saying, 'Buh-bye, she's not going to use us' "—has made her consider other options. "I'm at this weird place I never thought I'd be, where I'm considering having a child by myself, either naturally or through adoption," she said.

These decisions have serious financial and social implications—and SWANS don't take them lightly.

Jessica, 35, said she never really thought one way or another about having children, but now as she gets older, she values her time to herself. "Sharing is very difficult. I'm a very generous and sensitive person, and children are such a huge commitment, and I would take it so seriously that it would be a lot." She imagines that if she does have a child, it will be on her own. "I think a sell-out is when you say 'I want to have a baby, this guy is ready to have a baby, and oh, by the way, sure, I love him.' No, no, no, that's a recipe for disaster for me. I'd rather do it on my own.

"I would consider adopting or in vitro. I would consider not only babies, but adopting infants to 5," said Jessica. "I would do that when I definitively decide that I want to have children. With or without a spouse."

Dr. Howe, the Massachusetts infertility specialist, applauds thinking like Jessica's. He said many women forget the best option for having children later in life: adoption. "One has to question why patients are willing to spend years of painful procedures for something that is 5, 10, 20 percent possible. Adoption is a 98 percent chance of success."

Dr. Howe and his wife adopted a baby girl from South Korea when they were both 45. Now 49, Dr. Howe said it was "absolutely the right choice" for them. He encourages his patients to consider adoption early on in their decision-making process.

Race and Culture

For black and Latina SWANS, having a baby alone has cultural implications. More black and Latino children are born to single mothers than are born to white mothers, and for high-achieving minorities, being a single mom often carries a social stigma.

"I have a lot of friends who are single mothers. I made a conscious decision not to do that," said Hope, a 30-year-old black executive in Los Angeles. "I want my child to have a father. I don't want to set my child up not to have a father—but I might consider adopting one day. And when I date men, I do think about what kind of father they would be," she said. "I just have faith that when I'm ready to get pregnant, I will. My family, though, is putting pressure on me to have kids. Their pressure on me is more intense than the pressure on myself."

Her coworker Lola, a 29-year-old Latina, agreed. "I wouldn't have a child on my own. My family life gave me a lot of opportunities, but I don't think I could do it on my own." Lola recently got divorced and said she does feel the pressure to meet someone and start building a family, but she's not very concerned. "I want to have four kids, a big family, and I know I'm getting a little late. Hey, I just got *out of* a marriage," she said, laughing.

"I definitely think it's important to have a child by 35," said Madeline, 31, who is also divorced. "And I'm positive I will find someone special by then. But if I don't have a kid by 33, I might have a child with my ex-husband." Madeline said she recently met an amazing man, and if that relationship goes well, it would meet her biological time line. "I wouldn't share my time line with him, but it's good that he wants children. I'm looking for that."

For Kama, a 28-year-old management consultant and Indian American, having a child on her own would be culturally frowned upon. Plus, she said, her own family experiences have given her a firsthand look at how much work it is to raise a family on your own. "A few older girlfriends are considering going to a sperm bank, but watching my mother raise three kids under 13 after my dad died, I couldn't do it," she said.

Especially for high-achieving black women, the struggle to both meet a man and have children by a certain age seems too daunting. Adrianna, 42, said she's looking forward to having children—either by having a child on her own, through adoption, or marrying a man who has children from a previous relationship. "I really don't need a husband to give me things, I just need the hugs and the hold," she said. "I come from a career family where education is very important. You get your career set so you don't need to depend on anyone when you have a child. That's what I've done, but I think I did it a little too long."

Childless by Choice

For other high-achievers, children just aren't a priority. "Most women want to be married and have kids, but I'm not most women," said Patricia, a 32-year-old attorney. "I don't feel any need to be married. And kids may or may not be in the future." Other women agreed: One said she "never had the maternal instinct"; another said, "It just wasn't my thing." Elaine, a 42-year-old magazine journalist, said, "The whole marriage and babies thing was what we all wanted to get away from."

Having children isn't the be-all and end-all for high-achievers in their 20s and 30s. Eighty-eight percent of high-achieving women—and 92 percent of single high-achieving women—said they agreed with the statement "A person can lead a satisfying life without having children."

Had you asked these women about babies and family when they were in high school or in their first years of college, they might have given a different answer. In their teens and early 20s, before they created adult identities of their own and made their own choices, many of these women would have given the socially expected answer: Yes, I want to have children.

Several researchers point to this difference as the mark of failure: These women really wanted children and are simply rationalizing their choices by saying now that they didn't ever want to have a family. But the reality requires far less pop psychology analysis. As Oxford professor Avner Offer argues: "Although children are desirable, they also involve a sacrifice. The more highly educated the mother, the greater her sacrifice in terms of earnings and job satisfaction."[13] My new Harris Interactive opinion data support this: Only 66 percent of single non-high-achieving women agreed that a person could live a satisfying life without children—a striking difference from the 92 percent of high-achieving single women who agreed with that statement. These successful, educated women have myriad choices. And for the millions of high-achieving married women, having children is a choice.

For Jody, a 31-year-old research scientist, the decision to have children was made early. "At 23 I thought about kids. I was traveling in the United States for two weeks alone and I thought about my timetable: If I were going to have a faculty position by my mid-30s, I'd need to get kids out of the way in my early 30s . . . and I'd need to be married to the guy by 30," she said. "I got stressed out. It didn't seem feasible, and I accepted the idea that I'd never have kids. Yeah, I thought about all this at 23. And when I got back from my trip, my boyfriend said I had changed. He said I seemed more relaxed. I *was* more relaxed."

Balancing Careers and Children

Deborah, 31, looked down at her ever-expanding belly and wondered what the future would bring. Six months pregnant, she was anticipating some major life changes ahead. She and her husband live in a one-bedroom apartment in New York City and are debating a move to the suburbs. Because she is the breadwinner for the family, after her maternity leave, Deborah will go back to work full-time and hire a nanny to take care of the baby during the day.

"My whole life is going to change with this baby. I work nine a.m. to seven p.m., with a fair amount of travel," Deborah said, adding that her husband would be home each night at five to be with the baby—and she expects him to take on an equal, if not greater, share of the child rearing. "I definitely see him as being a great dad. I think he'll be a much better dad than I will be a mom."

For Deborah, children were always part of the plan. "I didn't think about a career when I was a kid. I just thought about family and getting married. I never had a drive to be an astronaut or anything specific," she said modestly. After business school, Deborah landed a top position at a technology firm and her career, despite her childhood expectations, took off. Now she earns 30 percent more than her husband and said he is very proud of her career success. "Sometimes it's funny when he comes to a business event with me because he'll say, 'Oh, you're the big executive,' and it's kind of amusing to him, but not intimidating. And we're a good pair: He enjoys cooking and cleaning and being around the home. As I said, he'll be a great dad."

Although few people will come out and say it these days, there's an ugly bias against successful women: Can you be an achiever and a good mother? SWANS report that they feel the need to tell men about their desires and plans to balance career and family early on in the dating process, lest men get the wrong impression.

"Do guys go into dating thinking they want to find a woman who will be a good mother to their children, or do they look for someone who they will have fun with?" wondered Raquel, 25, who works in private equity. "A guy at work was surprised that I wanted to have children. . . . He said I was so 'tough.' But listen, we're so young. Are these guys looking for a breeding machine, or are they looking for a life partner?

"When do I want to have kids?" Raquel laughs. "It gets pushed back as I get older. When I was younger I thought I'd be married by

28 and done having kids at 32. Now being married at 30 seems OK. Kids sometime after that."

High-achieving women are torn over the decision to work outside the home full-time, part-time, or not at all when they have children. If money were no object, 63 percent of high-achieving women in my Harris Interactive survey said they would want to stay at home with their children. But this statistic needs to be taken with several grains of salt.

First, some 60 percent of high-achieving men said the same thing: If money were no object, they would want to stay home and raise kids. So these data shouldn't be read as a signal that women aren't interested in gainful employment outside the home, any more than it should be read as a barometer of the career desires of men. Instead, it's an indication that both sexes are conscious of the balancing act that having a career and a family often entails.

Second, national surveys repeatedly underscore the fact that women enjoy their jobs. A 2002 Catalyst survey found that 67 percent of women in dual-career marriages would continue working whether or not they needed the money.[14] Working outside the home is a source of self-esteem, pride, and accomplishment for millions of American women.

Third, the vast majority of women with children *do* work outside the home, even among the well-educated and those who earn top salaries. Staying home full-time is an option only for the most wealthy of high-earning couples.

But this isn't what we read in the media recently. A front-page story in the *New York Times* reported that "many women at the nation's most elite colleges . . . will put aside their careers in favor of raising children."[15] Just over half of the women in their early 40s who had attended Yale said work was their primary activity, the article reported.

This may be true for Yale alumnae, but it certainly isn't true for the larger group of successful women nationally. This is a key point that runs counter to dozens of recent media reports about well-educated women opting out of the workforce.

Among high-achieving married women with children surveyed for this book, 93 percent were employed or self-employed. A full 64 percent of high-achieving women with children work *more than* 40 hours per week.

The very affluent have always had the luxury of choosing to work or not. But it's a mistake to generalize the choices of this tiny subset of America to all successful women. Elitist stories like the *New York Times* analysis of Yale graduates send the wrong message to the millions of women who will one day balance both career and family.

Heather Boushey, an economist at the Center for Economic and Policy Research in Washington, DC, was so frustrated by these negative media reports that she tested the theory of the opt-out revolution based on national data. She found that it was more a media creation than a statistical reality.

According to up-to-date Bureau of Labor Statistics data, Boushey finds that mothers with children are more likely to be in the labor force today than 20 years ago. In 1984, labor participation by women with children at home was 20.7 percentage points less than for women without children at home. In 2004, that penalty has diminished to 8.2 percentage points.

High-achieving mothers are advantaged compared to other mothers, not only in education and earnings potential, but they are more likely to be married—and married to a spouse with high earnings potential. Boushey finds that 91.2 percent of mothers with advanced degrees are married, compared with 78.3 percent of all mothers ages 25 to 44.

Boushey reports that nearly 8 out of 10 women with a graduate degree who have a child under the age of 18 at home are in the labor force, which is a higher percentage of work participation than for all other educational groups in that age range. "In short," she writes, "the overwhelming majority of thirty-something women with advanced degrees do not opt out if they have kids, but if they do opt out, they have kids." [16]

Educated and successful women are in the best position to balance children and a career. In part, this high level of workforce participation is a result of the intelligent choices that high-achieving women have made in order to balance their career and family. Kristen, 27, who works at a top financial group, said she's recently been asking herself some serious questions about the future: "How am I going to balance work with personal goals and kids?"

Kristen and Melissa have been friends since childhood, and this is a common topic these days. "If I got married and start having kids, I'd like to be there for my kids, and try to find something part-time, using my master's in international relations to do research, or something like that. But now that I'm going back into finance, I'm not sure. Maybe I'd take a few years off and then go back part-time," Kristen said.

Melissa, 26, agreed: "Trying out something in the arts would be my dream job in general and also a fairly flexible position. But I'm not sure I'll be challenged in the same way I was in finance, and I'm not sure how that will work for me."

Recently Melissa was accepted to an art program sponsored by a major auction house, and she is hoping to make a career switch from finance to the nonprofit world. "I would be lying if I said that [motherhood] wasn't a slight consideration [for doing the art program]. I love the way my mom was home when we got home from school. She helped us with our homework and she was always a great support. I would love to be able to do that, but also have something else, and the art world might be flexible."

Kristen believes she'll stay in finance for a few more years. She can imagine herself working right up until she has children, but after that, future plans get fuzzy. "At some point you have to make a decision. But it's a little bit of a scary thing. Are you going to end up like that MasterCard commercial with the woman talking baby-talk all day? That's sort of scary."

Melissa nodded, but said she is optimistic that there is a middle ground. "In 20 years I hope I'll have some kids and be married and working full-time." Kristen was less convinced. "I'll have kids. I'm not sure I'll be working, but I could do volunteer stuff."

For working mothers, the transition is often rocky. But Ruth, 35, said she's been able to make it work. "I have a 2-year-old daughter. And nothing prepared me for being a parent," she said. "I don't know how to cook. I felt unprepared. I had to completely relearn my work habits."

After her daughter was born, Ruth, who works at a nonprofit in Boston, said she had a "major meltdown" as she tried to juggle the demands of her job and her newborn. She couldn't sleep at night because her mind was racing—she always felt there was more that needed to be done. "The doctor said my body was telling me that I didn't have time for everything, so I couldn't sleep. It was awful."

Ruth took some time off to get back on track, and then resumed her full-time job. To encourage her to stay on at her job, her organization allowed her to work from home occasionally and have more flexible hours. "I always wanted to work at a nonprofit. Now it makes sense on two levels," she said. Her husband, a lawyer, has been very supportive. "He does a lot more than my friends' husbands. You just can't have two people full-out in their careers without a lot of help."

Carrie, a 42-year-old vice president at a major financial firm, couldn't agree more. She lives in San Francisco with her husband and 5-year-old daughter. After her daughter was born, Carrie worked as a freelancer until her daughter started preschool, and then she returned to a full-time job outside the home.

"I'm less clear on what professional success means. I used to think I'd have a certain title and responsibility to be successful, but my perspective changed after I had my daughter," Carrie said. "Because of the work and family balance, it's whatever works for you and what satisfies you. Whatever combination you can put together for yourself." Carrie's husband is a realtor and is able to both drop off and pick up their daughter from school each day. Carrie said his flexible schedule is an important component to making their family work.

Daddy Desire

For some married high-achieving women, pressure to have children is coming from the inside: Many husbands say they are ready to be fathers, or want a second child, before the women are ready.

"He wanted to have kids earlier, but I wanted to put it off for my career," said Carrie. "I wanted to get a manager position so I could more easily shift into consulting."

The financial burden also increases. "I'm not sure we have the money for another child. My husband wants one—and I've said, 'When you bring $40,000 more into this house, we can have another child,'" said Dawn, a Los Angeles executive.

Highly educated and high-earning men are significantly more likely to have children than less-educated, lower-earning men.[17] These types of men are traditionally seen as the most socially "desirable" mates who also have the financial strength to be able to support a family where either the mother stays home or works and uses the extra cash to pay for quality child care. But the majority of families—even high-achiever couples—don't have the luxury of these assumptions, and the biological truth is that having a child is usually a greater burden—both in terms of physical energy and time—for a mother than for a father. Ruth said her husband is thrilled about the baby she's expecting in a few months, but the news that she was pregnant was tough for her to take at first. "I was devastated initially when I found out I was pregnant. I do all these activities after work: photography classes, book club, going out with my friends. I just don't want to come straight home. I cried for weeks because that's all going to change. I've always wanted children—more than one, in fact—but the reality of it is pretty overwhelming."

For Jackie, a 30-year-old Type-A achiever, even thinking about taking nine months to be pregnant seems like a struggle. "I'm not sure I want to get off my career track," she said. "But David wants to be a father—and would have liked to have been a father by the time he was 35. But he's 34 now, so it's not happening, and he brings it up." Jackie's husband was a private asset manager who recently quit his job to write books full-time. And it's David who would have primary caretaking responsibilities for any children that the couple might have.

Many of David's friends are having children, and Jackie said that has increased the pressure on her. Adoption seems like a better option: "Then there's less pressure about this. I'd say 35 seems reasonable."

Jackie's sister is 34 and is retiring from her hard-charging career to start a family—and this is an option Jackie thinks about for herself. "She works more than I do, and both she and her husband are quitting their jobs to relax and have kids. She sees that her hours are affecting her marriage and she's chosen the marriage. It's not the decision for me right now, but someday I may be making that choice.

"There's a transition to marriage, and the hard thing is the guilt complex, not spending enough time together. The directors of my company who are married and have kids, you feel like they are always compromising. I believe you can't have everything," she said.

If the couple does have a child, Jackie said she is comfortable with the idea of David as Mr. Mom. "I don't want my kids to grow up knowing a nanny better than me, but I wouldn't mind if they were closer to my husband. I've got to keep working. Otherwise, how do you teach the value of work to your kids?"

Stay-at-Home Dads

An astounding 60 percent of high-achieving men in my Harris Interactive survey said they would like to stay home and raise the kids if money were not a concern. "I have no problem with the Mr. Mom role for some period of time. I've seen a lot of messed-up kids raised by nannies, so I really don't want that," said Kevin, a business school student.

But, as it is for their female counterparts, it's a question of money: "If I married a woman who made three times what I did, I'd be fine with being Mr. Mom, with part-time work on the side," said Tucker, a 32-year-old consultant. (Of course, to make three times his salary, a woman would have to be earning more than half a million dollars each year.)

There are varying estimates about the number of stay-at-home dads in America, but the number is certainly rising. According to recent census data, fathers are the primary caregivers for more than 20 percent of preschoolers in married-couple households.[18] And these current stay-at-home dads are providing role models for younger men. "One woman I work with, her husband runs a sales force recruiting firm out of their home and is a stay-at-home dad, and she works full-time. And that works. I wouldn't have an issue with it as long as I didn't feel like I sacrificed my career to be a telemarketer or something," said Michael, a 26-year-old in private equity.

"That's not something that I really think about when I think about getting married and having kids," said Nick. "But if she wanted to do it, I wouldn't have any problem with that. I could be a pretty good Mr. Mom. I do . . . think that if I'd be fortunate enough to be able to do that it would be kind of a nice thing to do.

"The idea that one parent would stay at home is a nice idea," Nick continued. "But if she wanted to work, by no means is that a deal breaker for me. And in that case, it might even encourage me to consider staying home for a while."

While high-achieving men express some openness to the idea of staying home and providing primary caretaking roles for their children, women are more ambivalent about this arrangement— and many are downright opposed to it.

Sherrie, a 27-year-old who works at a Chicago private equity firm, and Rebecca, a 32-year-old New Yorker, are far more certain that this is not the future they envision: "If one of us has to stay home, it'll be me. The whole house-husband thing doesn't work. But I'd like to work part-time at least," said Sherrie.

"No, seriously," said Rebecca. "It's become almost merely a dating weed-out question. You . . . pose some sort of hypothetical question like 'So what if your partner is more successful than you?' and a lot of time the unsolicited answer you get is 'I'll stay home with the kids.' They don't have children! You don't have any children in the hypothetical kingdom. They are volunteering to sit on their backside. 'Here, I'll just quit,' he says. It's the first instinct, and it's not cool," she said. "I think that they . . . feel, 'Hey, no problem, I'll take a break.' It's all what they hear about the whole glamour-puss existence, the Yummy Mummy generation of going to spas and hanging out with their friends. They are like, 'Shoot! I can do that. That seems enjoyable.'"

Rebecca said she's watching one of her close friends struggle with this issue now. She is a vice president at a large company and makes well into six figures; her husband just finished his medical residency and has been working difficult hours for little pay for years. So he recently decided to take some time off. "She's just like 'Wait! I didn't sign up for this. He's a doctor, for gosh sakes! Who thinks a doctor is going to sit on his butt?' I sympathize with her point. I mean, it must be very, very unusual to feel like you are with somebody who is a professional who seems by all accounts very motivated and ambitious in their career and, given an opportunity, . . . hangs out in a bean-bag chair. It's like, 'Oh! Wait a sec. Hang on!' I don't know that it's the right answer. I mean the idea of helping to raise children I think is very attractive. But it's like 'Let me quit my job and shop for things for the household'? No. That's not working. For the same reason I'm guessing that a woman who goes to the spa a lot and isn't contributing to the household isn't so attractive either."

Herding the Flock

If asked to predict the future, most SWANS say they expect their husband to be an equal partner in raising children and seem certain that they will be able to find the balance between fulfilling work and raising a family. "I'm certain I'd work, but I'm also certain I'd do the primary parenting" is an often repeated phrase.

What we think the future will look like doesn't always match up with reality. Still, many SWANS thinking about their multiple future roles as mother, wife, and career woman insist they will be both primary caregivers and work outside the home while their child is young.

But there can be only one primary caregiver, one person who is responsible for the day-to-day feeding, rearing, and playtime on any given afternoon. Most SWANS said they would want to take that role themselves, but in reality, nannies and day care providers are the norm as women move in and out of the workforce during their children's early years.

According to my new research, 35 percent of high-achieving women without children said if they were to have children they would envision themselves as the primary daytime caregiver. Another 32 percent said they would use day care primarily. Of women with children, 44 percent are the primary daytime caregivers, and 21 percent use day care. These numbers are fairly consistent with national data for all women.[19]

Many families combine day care, help from relatives, and the flexible schedule of one parent to make it work. "When my daughter was born, I started consulting, and when she was 4 years old, I started my current job at [a major credit card company]. Working as a consultant, I had three days at home and I traveled a lot on the other days, and we had a full-time nanny while I was away," said Carrie, who currently works full-time as a high-level executive now that her daughter has started kindergarten.

Deborah, pregnant with her first child, said she and her husband have discussed many alternatives, but money is the biggest issue. She makes more money than he does, but not enough to support the whole family. As with the majority of high-achievers—and the majority of Americans—both salaries are necessary to finance family life.

"I'm going to take three months off for maternity leave and then go back to work. If we had the money, my husband would stay home and raise our kids," said Deborah. "He enjoys cooking and cleaning and says he would like to stay home, but if it came down to it, I'm not sure he would. Anyway, we'll have a full-time nanny, and then he's going to take care of the baby after work, since his job is nine to five. I travel a lot, and he's the family guy."

High-achieving women who work full-time do feel the tension between their career and motherhood. "We have a nanny, but you feel like if you aren't there, they don't know you," said Ruth, who has a 2-year-old daughter. Yet, she said, "I never considered staying at home."

Early on in their careers—and for some, well before Mr. Right has come along—SWANS begin thinking about how to craft the best balance they can between career and family. For most, it's through flexible, creative careers or starting a business of their own.

In fact, since the mid-1990s, women have started their own companies at a rate twice the national average.[20]

Cynthia, 35, recently started her own event-planning company in San Francisco. "Part of the reason I quit corporate America and started my own firm was to spend time with my kids. And a nanny would be ideal if we could afford it. I need to continue working in some capacity," she said.

Kama said she wants to raise her children herself, at least for the first few years. "And yes, you're still a high-achiever if you choose to do that. It doesn't change your ability to contribute—it changes the way you choose to contribute."

So what do I do now? Advice to SWANS

High-achieving women marry at the same rate as all other women. There's no "success penalty" for young SWANS today.

Yet nearly half of high-achieving women said they believed a woman's career or educational success was holding her back in her search for Mr. Right, according to my new Harris Interactive data.

So if SWANS get married at the same rate as all other women, why do they perceive themselves to be at a disadvantage?

- *Because dating is difficult. It usually takes a lot of dull, strange, or even painful dating experiences to meet Mr. Right. That's true for all women, but it always seems worse when it's* your *personal life. For SWANS who marry later, it means more years of dating Mssrs. Not-Quite-Right. So when the going gets tough, we need an excuse: How about that we're too fabulous, too smart, and too successful?*

- **Because for our mother's and grandmother's generations, successful women were less likely to get married.** *This generation of SWANS is the first for whom being ambitious and accomplished can actually be an asset rather than a liability in the mating game.*

- **Because the media love bad news.** *Think about the last article you saw on successful women. Odds are it was negative—and not representative of your life because it was based on a small or outdated sample of women. Perhaps it was a lament that high-IQ women don't get married? A piece about how well-educated women are opting out to have children? This isn't true for SWANS, but with all the coverage these bad news pieces get, it's no wonder that high-achieving women are depressed.*

SWANS need to get past these excuses, out-of-date information, and bad news.

- **Success isn't what's holding you back in your dating life, but your bad attitude might be.** *Sixty-five percent of single men said they are more attracted to women who are successful in their careers. Remarkably, men's attitudes toward SWANS have progressed farther than have the SWANS' attitudes toward themselves.*

- **Be honest about your achievements and who you are.** *Don't lie and tell a man you are a stewardess when you are actually finishing your doctoral work. It's insulting to everyone. If you are lighthearted and fun, if he's attracted to you and finds you* *interesting, a man won't care very much what you do. Getting to know someone isn't about comparing résumés. You wouldn't date a man just because he had a certain job or salary, so why would you assume he'd make such judgments about you?*

- **Ditch your Cinderella Complex.** *You are a successful, accomplished woman in your own right. You don't need to be rescued. Your success and accomplishments enable you to broaden your horizons in your search for a husband. The idea that you would only marry a man who has more education and makes more money than you do is antiquated—and might cause you to overlook your soul mate.*

- **Stop perpetuating this myth.** *There's a high cost to the conventional wisdom that accomplished women don't get married: Young women in high school and college who are contemplating graduate school or high-powered careers will think twice about pursuing their dreams if they are constantly bombarded with bad news about their prospects for love. For high-achieving women to take the next step toward equality, it's time to shake off these stereotypes.*

Chapter 9

Futures and Options

OLIVIA, 30, GAVE BIRTH to her son three days before her business school final exams. As she and her husband celebrate their fourth anniversary, she balances two children under age 2 and the growth of a boutique real estate firm in Connecticut that she founded last year. "This generation is more confused because we don't have set roles," Olivia said. "Even though I know I want a high-achieving career, I wonder how I can leave my children for 70 hours each week." She marvels at the other women in her neighborhood who work and volunteer. "These women run bake sales like Fortune 500 companies."

Olivia chose her career with an eye on family balance: "An entrepreneurial job allows me the time and flexibility to do both. I would be missing my kids growing up and sacrificing my relationship with my husband if I worked in finance. But you're never off duty. I'll put the kids down and work from seven to eleven p.m. I mix in family and work, I bring the kids to the city, and they go to the park with a nanny while I work."

Olivia and her husband have a full-time live-in nanny. She understands it's a luxury, but also feels that society judges her for it. "Having the nanny around means people question me as a mother.

I do bathtime and read them stories each night. I spend all weekend with them, and as much of the daytime during the week as I can. And my husband is home by seven or eight each night. He's a great father," she said. Still, she worries. "When highly educated women drop out to raise kids and your husband comes home and asks what you did today: You were with the kids. The talk is all about going to the gym and grocery store," she said. "But if you are out doing something else . . ." she trails off.

"If your career is your only identity, when you have kids you're going to get in trouble. I was afraid I'd lose my identity and become wife and mother, but I don't think I have. You can't define it that way."

Olivia captures the conflict that so many successful mothers face: "When I leave my kids and go to work, I cry for them. But at the same time, I've been so well educated and have so much to offer society, I should be in the workforce," she said. "Doesn't it make you selfish either way?"

Olivia's daughter is 5 months old, and her mother is already thinking about what the future will hold for her. She said she would tell her daughter, "You have to put yourself in the right situation to meet a man—and if you want to align yourself with a guy who wants a smart woman, then sure, you should go to grad school or medical school. But you have to have an identity before you can attract someone—and you can't go in just wanting to be a wife."

Olivia is one of the millions of women who shatters three of the most insidious myths about high-achieving women: that successful women don't get married, that accomplished women don't have children, and that well-educated women are opting out of the workforce.

As Olivia and dozens of other women in this book have said, it isn't easy: SWANS often spend years searching for their soul mates, and the balancing act between career and family takes stamina. But millions of American women are doing it.

SWANS Do *Get Married*

Since the 1970s, surveys have found that young Americans are increasingly committed to the institution of marriage and rank a happy union as a very important goal in their lives.[1] Indeed, a Catalyst study of men and women born between 1964 and 1974 found that 84 percent said it was "extremely important" to have a loving family, whereas only 21 percent said the same thing about earning a great deal of money.[2]

Surveys of high-achieving women report the same thing: Marriage is a priority for most SWANS—and an attainable goal. Among women ages 35 to 39, 88 percent with graduate degrees have married. Even among uber-high-achieving urban women—women earning $100,000 or more each year, who live in a city with a population of 1 million or more—nearly 90 percent are married in the 30–44 age group.

So it's no wonder that when SWANS think about their future, they envision a future that involves marriage—and perhaps children. "In 10 years I see myself married, and probably with kids, in an executive position at a nonprofit," said Melanie, a 26-year-old business student in Washington, DC. Alexis, 35, predicted a similar scenario for herself: "In 10 or 15 years I see myself married and raising kids, doing something like designing and building furniture. I love the creative process," she mused. For Cynthia, 35, an ideal future is one that affords comfort, self-respect, and a balance of work and play. Looking 20 years ahead, she envisions herself "retired with a couple of kids in their teens. We'll be enjoying life and maximizing the time that we have together. We'll be very comfortable financially, and I'll be comfortable with who I am physically. I want to be able to be happy and look back and say that the twists of life were all for a reason."

Michele

Recently, Michele and Dan spent the early evening at their local New York City bar. After his dog-walking rounds, Dan had gone food shopping for eggs, nutmeg, onions, and the makings of a fresh crust for the quiche that he and Michele were having for dinner. When Michele came home, she helped Dan put the finishing touches on the eggy masterpiece, and into the oven it went while the couple headed out for a beer.

Married for nearly six years, Michele and Dan are bonded as a team. Michele recently received a major promotion at the investment services company she works at and is bringing in a large paycheck. Dan's dog-walking company on the Upper West Side of Manhattan has him spending each day in Central Park with his furry clients. With the help of Michele's business acumen, his earnings have increased more than 500 percent in the past two years.

Mornings are the times that Dan and Michele treasure: Dan makes the coffee and gets the paper, Michele goes for a run, and they watch the *Today* show before she heads into the office. On weekends, the couple curls up with the *New York Times* real estate section; they are looking to buy an apartment soon.

"My work is fairly insane, but it's not my life, so I really try to separate being driven from being married. I married someone who is so relaxed, he's so opposite from me. When I get home we sit down and talk and have a glass of wine, and it slows me down in a great way," Michele said.

"If someone wants to change you and make you into something that they desire—why don't you want to be with someone who wants you? I don't get that. I want someone who wants me. I don't want someone who wants that girl over there."

Neither Michele nor Dan wanted to have children of their own. It was something they discussed early in their relationship, but Michele said they might consider adopting in the future. "I would love to rescue a child someday, but we can't do that right now. We're too busy, we have too much going on. Society expects you to be a nuclear family, but it's what you can handle, and you should never go beyond that if you want to stay sane." Dan added, "We have a five-year plan where Michele is going to collect five more bonuses and keep pulling in the big money, and I'm going to quadruple the dog-walking business so that Michele can come in and run it once she's finished in the corporate world."

"We get along really well, so this could be the ideal business to grow and give us income in the future—even into retirement," said Michele. "In 20 years I want to slow down. I want to be spending more time with Dan and my friends. These days, I come home stressed and he's relaxed. He'll cook, or since I love to cook, he'll do the grocery shopping and then we'll cook together.

"It's called contentment," Michele said.

The Real Story About Successful Women and Children

Married high-achieving women are just as likely to have children as their lesser-achieving married sisters. This generation of successful women is shattering the myth of the barren executive.

According to 2005 Census data, among married women who earn $60,000 per year or more, 73 percent have children—the same as married women who earn less. Among married women who have graduate degrees, 77 percent have children, making highly educated women slightly *more* likely to have children than women who have less education.

It's also incorrect to assume that successful women without children are yearning for babies. When women gained entrance into the executive suite, the decision to remain childless and seek fulfillment through their career and other aspects of their personal life became a much more attainable reality.

Still, the majority of SWANS see children in their futures. "I'm going to have three boys by the time I'm 44—who are actively involved in sports. I have great hopes for my unborn kids," said Shayna, a medical resident in New York. Her friend and fellow medical resident, Nadia, agreed: "I see myself having three kids and being married." She added that she would consider taking time away from medicine to raise her kids while they were young and then would return as a private practice doctor.

For Dawn, a black advertising executive in Los Angeles who recently married after having a child with another man several years earlier, the future is in her daughter's hands. "I've started to write a letter to my daughter every year. 'This was a really good year,' I'll say in this first letter. 'Mommy got married to Daddy.' I have a really good life and I have no complaints. I want even better for her, too," Dawn said. "I think my daughter will be more likely to marry a high-achieving black man—or a man of any other race. It's getting better."

To make the future even brighter for their children, these high-achieving women understand that it's important to stop perpetuating the myth that success and love are mutually exclusive. By mentoring younger women and instilling in their own daughters a positive attitude toward career and family balance, today's ambitious women can make a lasting impact.

Antoinette

"I feel like I'm 12. I've never done this," said Antoinette, sounding giddy. "Am I too excited? Should this be a red flag? I have some women in my life—aside from my mother, who gets a little crazed—who are wonderful and who I can talk to. They keep it in perspective for me," she said. "It's all really good. I'm so happy. But you know, I continue to think too much, and I think that's a problem with dating at a later age."

Antoinette will turn 40 in a few months and will be starting part-time classes for her MBA. And she and Luke are talking about marriage. "We talked about marriage a few weeks ago," she said. "We were just talking about things . . . when we both agreed we would want to sell my house and use the equity in the house to buy another, older house that he could fix up.

"We talked about a wedding, and how I wanted my church minister, not my dad, to marry me. We talked about big versus small weddings, and where we might have it. Outside versus inside, and who we would invite. We'd probably have it in the summer when he's not as busy.

"And we talked about having kids. He's 45 and I'll be 40 soon. Before, I decided I didn't want to have kids. Ever since I was in my late 20s, I never wanted to have children. But now that I met him, part of me wants to have kids with him. We talked about what a great dad he would be. We're talking about boys—twins, he has a twin gene.

"Luke is the kind of man who would be an at-home dad in a minute. I'm not Sally Homemaker. I'm not ever going to be that woman who wants to stay home. But on some levels, it's him. Plus, he already has two kids, so either way, I guess I might get some.

"We were talking about our future in terms of how we don't like being apart. Even if I'm in a bad mood, this is where I want to be," she said. "When we argue, he doesn't leave. He may leave the space that I'm in, but he doesn't leave the relationship. It's very mature, which is refreshing. We can be upset and have a disagreement and get it back together."

As their one-year anniversary approaches, Antoinette and Luke are in constant discussions about the future. "March was madness and April will bring about the change in my life that spring carries with it anyway," she said, smiling, and fully aware that she was dropping tantalizing hints about some big news to come. "Who knows what will happen in May."

Juggling It All

In the 1950s, 25 percent of all wives worked outside the home. In the early 1990s, the rate was up to 58 percent of married women, and nearly two-thirds of married women with children.[3] According to my new research, 93 percent of married high-achieving women with children were employed or self-employed. And a full 64 percent of high-achieving women with children work *more than* 40 hours per week.

High-achieving women are not opting out of the workforce in the droves that recent media reports would have us believe. Although leaving the workforce to raise a family has been—and continues to be—an attractive option among the most affluent, the majority of well-educated, high-earning women aren't making these choices.

Newly published research from sociologists at Pennsylvania State University finds that, contrary to conventional wisdom, wives' full-time employment is associated with greater marital stability.[4] According to marriage historian Stephanie Coontz, working mothers and their children do best when the women are "skilled, long-term employees" who are respected by their employers for the assets they bring to their job. To get these kinds of jobs, a woman needs to invest in her education and her job skills: just what the young, high-achieving women of today are doing in their 20s and 30s.[5]

Smart, successful women realize that achieving these benefits does come at a cost—and balance is the word most often heard among young women hoping to juggle career and family.

Randi Minetor, author of *Breadwinner Wives and the Men They Marry*, said one reason successful women struggle in their relationships is because they try to do it all: "These women feel like they are saddled with the whole burden, supporting the household and doing the housework. Women are trapped in the mind-set that they have to run a good household as well as bring in all the money."

A woman's satisfaction in her role—as a worker, a homemaker, or whatever she chooses—is the best predictor of both a good relationship with her children and of the child's well-being.[6] And the good news is that more and more women are finding a balance that works for them—and they are more than happy to offer advice on how they are doing it.

At 35, pregnant with her second child, adorned in big jewelry and bubbling over with excitement about the growth of her multimillion-dollar event-planning company, Allegra is larger than life. Yet when it comes to her interactions with men, she said she is kitten soft and feminine. "Strong successful women are used to going after the client and achieving their goals, but with men you need to have a different closing strategy. The combination that goes wrong is the successful women who apply their business strategies to the dating world. Put on a pink fuzzy sweater and makeup, ladies, and be a girl."

Allegra was married at 22 to a man almost twice her age. They divorced several years later, after having one child, and Allegra hit the dating scene. "I always said I didn't want to get married—and I think that made men more interested. I hit that point where I was in my 30s, single, and I had to decide whether I was desperate or whether I was going to say 'I'm strong. Take it or leave it.' And I have always been a take-it-or-leave-it kind of girl." At 32 she married her current husband, 10 years her senior, and is looking forward to the arrival of their son. "And no, I won't stop working when I have the baby."

Allegra's husband earns 60 percent of the family income, but she said that's changing quickly as he leaves his peak earning years. "I've been doing some real estate stuff on the side and just netted $50,000 on a house last week. He went into a tailspin because he wants to be better, stronger, faster than me, but at the same time, he's also my biggest cheerleader.

"Things are getting better. The lines between men's and women's roles are starting to blur, but I don't think we're there yet. Just now you have generations of men raised by doctor and lawyer mothers—and they can date who they want and have a much more open view. That's where the changes will come." Still, she said, "I would advise women that men who are not gay want a woman, not a drill sergeant. He wants a wife, not a chief operating officer.

"I chose my career because it was something I loved to do and I was good at it. And I wanted to make money, so I needed a strategy to do that. Now, I tailor how hard I work based on all my other goals—including have a happy marriage, and a healthy, stable child." But balancing it all is a challenge: "I'm the primary caretaker of my kids. Ultimately, the woman has to know that it's up to her to figure it out. I multitask. I get a ton of help from everyone, including my ex-husband, but if my son is sick, I have to figure it out. If the plumber needs to be called, I'll do it."

Successful women need a plan, Allegra advised. "Panic isn't

going to solve the problem. I do think if you want to have a husband, make a million bucks, and have kids, you have to have a plan. It's hard to hit a target that you yourself can't see. But you don't need to communicate that plan on every date!" Once the plan is formulated, execute: "You can't sit on your bed and say 'I want my company to be a success' or 'I want a date.' You have to make it happen. Write down your goals, and be specific: These are the qualities I want in someone. And don't forget there is a lot to be said for compatibility: Does he have your back? Is he on your team?"

Most books of this sort end with a call for family-friendly work policies, affordable quality child care, flextime, and a wistful longing for Europe's family benefits. This used to really bother me. "Give me practical advice, not utopian dreams of social change," I'd mutter when I got to these final chapters.

Yet these broad-scale social changes *are* good ideas. America does need to improve the support network offered to both women *and* men who are starting families and striving for career success. Employers *do* need to establish their work policies on the assumption that both sexes will have active caretaking roles at various points in their career track.

What women *don't* need are mandates for how to live their lives.

In Sylvia Hewlett's controversial book on high-achieving women and children, *Creating a Life,* she ends with recommendations of five things women can do to "enhance their chances of creating the lives they want":

- Ask yourself what you want your life to look like at 45. If you see children in the picture, you need to become "seriously proactive."
- Give "urgent priority to finding a partner . . . in your twenties."

- Have your first child before 35.
- Choose a career that will allow you to have a more flexible schedule to enable the work-family balance.
- Choose an employer who will offer this kind of schedule.[7]

These are all good suggestions—but they aren't mandates, and they don't have to happen instantaneously in a woman's early 20s. Dozens of women interviewed and polled in the new research presented in this book married and had children later in life and changed jobs many times along the way. The choices offered to high-achievers today make life a choose-your-own-adventure novel, where every flip of the page unfolds new options. There are no right and wrong choices: Many women who follow none of these edicts go on to lead happy and fulfilled lives, and the reverse is true as well. Early marriage and child rearing don't always equate with happiness.

There's a lot of encouraging research to suggest a bright future, happy marriages, and an increasingly balanced reality of career and family life. But women in their 20s and 30s are just beginning their journey, so we'll have to watch and see what happens.

Christina

Christina and Josh were married by Christina's sister, a Unitarian minister. Christina walked down the aisle to Ella Fitzgerald singing "Night and Day," and the newlyweds exited the ceremony with the Beatles singing "All You Need Is Love." Christina was 35 and Josh was 36.

A few months before the wedding, Christina considered how fortunate she was. "I would not have married the same guy I married today if I had gotten married younger," she said. "And another benefit to me is that I can pay for my own wedding and do exactly what I want. . . . To me, the financial independence is independence generally.

"There's no other way to do [it]—to live the life that you want to live—than to earn your own money and pay your own way. If I were 24 and my parents were paying for my wedding, I would have my mother's wedding.

"And I've been saving my money, I have to admit," she said.

Christina's first savings account was for an apartment. At 32, she had enough saved and took the plunge. She bought a one-bedroom apartment in Manhattan. "That was the day I signed my name a million times and I was like, 'I'm always going to be single. I'm never going to get married. This is it for me.' . . . That to me was like this confirmation that I'd stopped waiting for a guy.

"I know many women who are my age and older who [say], 'I'm not buying my own apartment.' Buy an apartment. They say, 'No, because I want to get married,' and I'll tell them that they are out of their minds. You're making an investment. Yes, it's a big step, and yes, I had to really get myself to come to grips with my emotions and not make it about admitting defeat in the dating world. But this is about putting your money into real estate. It's just like buying mutual funds. You're doing the best thing for yourself. . . . I really did have to coerce myself to get to that frame of mind.

"So that was three years ago. And after that, I started putting more money aside and said, 'You know, if and when I ever get married, I'm paying for this wedding because I want this to be what I want.' And when we got engaged we started looking around and figuring out what we are going to do. . . . This is what I can afford. And he has some money from his parents that he can pitch in. And we're doing just what we want."

Christina and Josh have also worked out a way to share their finances in the future, and the two have talked it through openly. "We are going to each contribute the same amount to a shared household account, and we are going to define what is considered a shared expense. And that will be mortgage, maintenance, you know, cable, telephone, laundry, sundry items for the apartment. We'll try to budget an entertainment expense for movies, dinners out, whatever. So anything that is spent on ourselves will come out of our own [accounts], but anything that's our shared expense comes out of our joint account. We don't know what's going to work. We don't know how much we're going to need. We don't know what's going to be too much, what's going to be too little, so we're going to kind of take it, you know, the first few months and reevaluate it and see what's what. But we're talking about it all the time."

As for children, Christina and Josh are hopeful. "We've talked about it, of course, and we're, I think we're both in the 'Let's see if it happens' zone. And if it happens, great, and if it doesn't, we're not going to freak out. We're definitely going to give it a go." They'd like to be married for one year and "settled" before having a baby, but they are going to officially start trying soon.

Christina laughs at the number of people who ask her if she's going to have a baby now that she and Josh are married. "I want to tell all of them, 'When I ask for a club soda, you'll know, but please don't ask me!' We're really happy. We'll just see what happens."

Appendix

Harris Interactive Survey

Below are selected results from two Harris Interactive surveys, specially commissioned for this book, of more than 3,700 Americans. In January 2006, a nationally representative group of 1,629 high-achieving men and women ages 25–40 participated in the first survey, followed in May 2006 by an omnibus survey of a nationally representative group of 2,073 adult Americans. Because of rounding, some sections do not add up to 100 percent.

How successful do you consider yourself?

	WOMEN		MEN	
	Single	*Married*	*Single*	*Married*
Very Successful/Successful	90%	94%	86%	95%
Very Unsuccessful/ Unsuccessful	10%	6%	14%	5%

How satisfied are you with your life?

	WOMEN		MEN	
	Single	*Married*	*Single*	*Married*
Extremely/Very Satisfied	29%	57%	36%	56%
Satisfied	41%	28%	41%	31%
Somwhat Satisfied/Not at All Satisfied	30%	15%	23%	13%

One can live a fulfilling, happy life regardless of whether one is married.

	HIGH-ACHIEVING				NON-HIGH-ACHIEVING			
	WOMEN		MEN		WOMEN		MEN	
	Single	Married	Single	Married	Single	Married	Single	Married
Strongly Agree/ Agree	94%	90%	85%	83%	91%	90%	91%	69%
Strongly Disagree/ Disagree	6%	10%	15%	17%	9%	10%	9%	31%

I would prefer to be married to/married someone who is as committed to their career as I am.

	WOMEN		MEN	
	Single	Married	Single	Married
Strongly Agree/Agree	76%	65%	68%	54%
Strongly Disagree/Disagree	24%	35%	32%	46%

Men are more attracted to women who are successful in their careers.

	WOMEN		MEN	
	Single	Married	Single	Married
Strongly Agree/Agree	64%	59%	65%	55%
Strongly Disagree/Disagree	36%	41%	35%	45%

I find it hard to meet people I would be interested in dating or having a relationship with.

	Single Women	Single Men
Strongly Agree/Agree	76%	74%
Strongly Disagree/Disagree	24%	26%

I don't have enough time for my personal life.

	WOMEN		MEN	
	Single	*Married*	*Single*	*Married*
Strongly Agree/Agree	43%	43%	51%	53%
Strongly Disagree/Disagree	57%	57%	49%	47%

It is easier to have a good relationship when just one person has a high-powered career.

	WOMEN		MEN	
	Single	*Married*	*Single*	*Married*
Strongly Agree/Agree	23%	33%	36%	38%
Strongly Disagree/Disagree	77%	67%	64%	62%

I'm not waiting to get married. I'm living my life to the fullest now.

	Single Women	*Single Men*
Strongly Agree/Agree	81%	60%
Strongly Disagree/Disagree	19%	40%

Women who are stay-at-home parents are better mothers than women who work outside the home.

	WOMEN		MEN	
	Single	*Married*	*Single*	*Married*
Strongly Agree/Agree	23%	19%	38%	50%
Strongly Disagree/Disagree	77%	81%	62%	50%

Did you think you would be married by now?

	Single Women	Single Men
Yes	64%	61%
No	36%	39%

Would you like to have more children/adopt more children?

	WOMEN		MEN	
	Single	Married	Single	Married
Yes	67%	61%	63%	49%
No	33%	39%	37%	51%

Have you ever used an online dating service?

	Single Women	Single Men
Yes	48%	55%
No	52%	45%

A woman's career or educational success makes her more desirable as a wife.

	WOMEN		MEN	
	Single	Married	Single	Married
Strongly Agree/Agree	85%	73%	74%	70%
Strongly Disagree/Disagree	15%	27%	26%	30%

Do you think women who have achieved career or educational success
are more, less, or as likely to get married?

| | HIGH-ACHIEVING | | | | NON-HIGH-ACHIEVING | | | |
| | WOMEN | | MEN | | WOMEN | | MEN | |
	Single	Married	Single	Married	Single	Married	Single	Married
More likely	7%	6%	3%	6%	10%	5%	8%	17%
Less likely	43%	30%	49%	42%	36%	33%	42%	38%
As likely	51%	64%	48%	52%	53%	62%	50%	45%

Do you think men who have achieved career or educational success are
more, less, or as likely to get married?

| | WOMEN | | MEN | |
	Single	Married	Single	Married
More likely	60%	46%	49%	49%
Less likely	7%	6%	6%	6%
As likely	33%	47%	45%	45%

Thinking about the various qualities or characteristics you look for in a
potential/that describe your spouse, please rate the following.

INTELLIGENT

	All Women	Single Women	All Men	Single Men
More	21%	21%	25%	27%
As	73%	79%	64%	73%
Less	5%	–	11%	1%

AMBITIOUS

	All Women	Single Women	All Men	Single Men
More	23%	28%	26%	19%
As	58%	72%	50%	66%
Less	19%	1%	24%	15%

Appendix

ACCOMPLISHED

	All Women	Single Women	All Men	Single Men
More	19%	23%	19%	16%
As	64%	77%	60%	81%
Less	16%	–	21%	2%

CAPABLE OF EARNING A GOOD INCOME

	All Women	Single Women	All Men	Single Men
More	31%	36%	23%	24%
As	60%	63%	56%	73%
Less	8%	–	21%	3%

KIND AND UNDERSTANDING

	All Women	Single Women	All Men	Single Men
More	26%	24%	46%	35%
As	66%	75%	49%	65%
Less	8%	–	5%	–

PHYSICALLY ATTRACTIVE

	All Women	Single Women	All Men	Single Men
More	15%	14%	44%	46%
As	80%	85%	53%	54%
Less	6%	–	3%	–

I would be open to marrying someone who has less education than I do.

	HIGH-ACHIEVING		NON-HIGH-ACHIEVING	
	Single Women	Single Men	Single Women	Single Men
Strongly Agree/Agree	84%	84%	72%	94%
Strongly Disagree/Disagree	16%	16%	28%	6%

I married someone who had less education than I had.

	Married Women	Married Men
True	54%	25%
False	46%	75%

I would be open to marrying someone who did not earn as much money as me.

	HIGH-ACHIEVING		NON-HIGH-ACHIEVING	
	Single Women	Single Men	Single Women	Single Men
Strongly Agree/Agree	82%	99%	89%	96%
Strongly Disagree/Disagree	18%	1%	11%	4%

I married someone who did not earn as much money as me.

	Married Women	Married Men
True	33%	61%
False	67%	39%

I would be open to marrying someone who is of a different religious background or faith.

	Single Women	Single Men
Strongly Agree/Agree	74%	77%
Strongly Disagree/Disagree	26%	23%

I married someone who is of a different religious background or faith.

	Married Women	Married Men
True	37%	41%
False	63%	59%

I would be comfortable being the primary breadwinner/earner for my family.

	WOMEN		MEN	
	Single	*Married*	*Single*	*Married*
Strongly Agree/Agree	61%	70%	86%	88%
Strongly Disagree/Disagree	39%	30%	14%	12%

I think my career or educational success is intimidating to men/women I meet.

	Single Women	*Single Men*
Strongly Agree/Agree	44%	23%
Strongly Disagree/Disagree	56%	77%

I tend to minimize my career or educational success in conversation when I first meet someone I might be interested in becoming involved with romantically.

	Single Women	*Single Men*
Strongly Agree/Agree	32%	47%
Strongly Disagree/Disagree	68%	53%

My parents would prefer to see me married to someone who earns at least as much money as I do.

	Single Women	*Single Men*
Strongly Agree/Agree	73%	22%
Strongly Disagree/Disagree	27%	78%

My parents would prefer to see me married to someone who has at least the same level of education as me.

	Single Women	Single Men
Strongly Agree/Agree	64%	54%
Strongly Disagree/Disagree	36%	46%

My parents will be disappointed if I do not get married.

	Single Women	Single Men
Strongly Agree/Agree	49%	57%
Strongly Disagree/Disagree	51%	43%

My career or educational success increases my chances of getting married.

	Single Women	Single Men
Strongly Agree/Agree	34%	60%
Strongly Disagree/Disagree	66%	40%

My friends are all getting married and I am worried about being left behind.

	Single Women	Single Men
Strongly Agree/Agree	33%	40%
Strongly Disagree/Disagree	67%	60%

Have you ever lost or become estranged from friends because you were at different phases of your life?

	Women	Men
Yes	84%	78%
No	16%	22%

A person can lead a satisfying life without having children.

	HIGH-ACHIEVING				NON-HIGH-ACHIEVING			
	WOMEN		MEN		WOMEN		MEN	
	Single	*Married*	*Single*	*Married*	*Single*	*Married*	*Single*	*Married*
Strongly Agree/ Agree	92%	87%	84%	79%	66%	73%	90%	67%
Strongly Disagree/ Disagree	8%	13%	16%	21%	34%	27%	10%	33%

If I had all the money I needed, I would be a stay-at-home parent.

	WOMEN		MEN	
	Single	*Married*	*Single*	*Married*
Strongly Agree/Agree	55%	68%	58%	61%
Strongly Disagree/Disagree	45%	32%	42%	39%

I am worried that I won't be able to have children.

	WOMEN		MEN	
	Single	*Married*	*Single*	*Married*
Strongly Agree/Agree	47%	48%	17%	28%
Strongly Disagree/Disagree	53%	52%	83%	72%

Smart women make better mothers.

	WOMEN		MEN	
	Single	*Married*	*Single*	*Married*
Strongly Agree/Agree	65%	62%	64%	69%
Strongly Disagree/Disagree	35%	38%	36%	31%

Notes

INTRODUCTION

1 Catalyst, "Quick Takes: Women in Their 20s & 30s" (New York: Catalyst, Inc., 2005).

CHAPTER 1: MEET THE SWANS

1 Stephanie L. Brown and Brian P. Lewis, "Relational Dominance and Mate Selection Criteria: Evidence That Males Attend to Female Dominance," *Evolution and Human Behavior* 25 (2004).

2 The data for this book come from a variety of different sources. U.S. Census and Current Population Survey data underpin the argument that today's successful, well-educated young women marry at the same rates as all other women. Harris Interactive survey data specially commissioned for this book provide information about the opinions, goals, and aspirations of high-achieving men and women. Other sources of data are clearly cited throughout the book.

3 Andrew Sum et al., "Growing Gender Gaps in College Enrollment and Degree Attainment in the U.S. and Their Potential Economic and Social Consequences" (Washington, DC: Prepared for the Business Roundtable by the Center for Labor Market Studies at Northeastern University, 2003), p. 38.

4 Ibid.

5 Ibid., p. 22.

6   Catalyst, "The Bottom Line: Connecting Corporate Performance and Gender Diversity" (New York: Catalyst, Inc., 2004).

7   Editor, "Marketing to the Affluent Woman," in *Neuberger Berman Research* (New York: Lehman Brothers Company, 2004); http://www.cfwbr.org/topfacts.html.

8   Ibid.

9   U.S. Census, "Marital Status of the Population by Sex and Age: 2004," in *America's Families and Living Arrangements 2004* (Washington, DC: U.S. Census Bureau, 2005).

10 Arland Thornton and Linda Young-DeMarco, "Four Decades of Trends in Attitudes Toward Family Issues in the United States: The 1960s Through the 1990s," *Journal of Marriage and the Family* 63 (November 2001), p. 1019.

11 Joann S. Lublin, "A Career Wife Complicates the CEO's Life," *Wall Street Journal,* December 15, 1994.

12 Julia Hollar quoted in Reyhan Harmanci, "Women's Pages: Next Time You Read About 'What Women Want,' Check the Research—It's Likely to Be Flimsy," *San Francisco Chronicle,* January 4, 2006.

13 Claudia Goldin, "Career and Family: College Women Look to the Past," in *Gender and Family Issues in the Workplace,* ed. Francine D. Blau and Ronald G. Ehrenberg (New York: Russell Sage Foundation, 1997), p. 30.

14 Elaina Rose, "Education and Hypergamy, and the 'Success Gap,'" working paper no. 53 (updated version of working paper no. 33, "Does Education Really Disadvantage Women in the Marriage Market?"), Center for Statistics and the Social Sciences at the University of Washington, 2005.

15 In June 2006, *Newsweek* published another cover story retracting their 1986 comments. See Daniel McGinn, "Marriage by the Numbers: Twenty Years Since the Infamous 'Terrorist' Line, States of Unions Aren't What We Predicted They'd Be," *Newsweek,* June 5, 2006.

16 Abigail Van Buren, "Smart Single Women Despair of Ever Finding True Love," uexpress.com, December 21, 2005.

Notes

CHAPTER 2: OVERQUALIFIED FOR LOVE?

1   Barbara Dafoe Whitehead, "The Plight of the High-Status Woman," *Atlantic Monthly,* December 1999.

2   "Men Prefer to Wed Secretary," UPI Newswires, December 13, 2004.

3   Editor, "Too Smart to Marry?," *Atlantic Monthly,* April 2005.

4   Melissa Kent, "Here Dumbs the Bride," *West Australian* (Perth), January 15, 2005; Ann Marie Hourihane, "Keep Young and Stupidful If You Want to Be Loved," *Sunday Tribune,* January 30, 2005; Editor, "Alpha Females Use Their Heads, but Lose Their Hearts," *Courier Mail,* March 1, 2005.

5   Sylvia Ann Hewlett, *Creating a Life: What Every Woman Needs to Know About Having a Baby and a Career* (New York: Hyperion, 2002), pp. 39 and 85.

6   Maureen Dowd, *Are Men Necessary? When Sexes Collide* (New York: Putnam, 2005), p. 48.

7   Maureen Dowd, "Powerful Male Looking for Maid to Marry," *International Herald Tribune,* January 14, 2005.

8   John Schwartz, "Glass Ceilings at Altar as Well as Boardroom," *New York Times,* December 14, 2004.

9   Editor, "They're Too Smart for These Guys," *Chicago Sun-Times,* December 15, 2004.

10 Michelle D. Taylor et al., "Childhood IQ and Marriage by Mid-Life: The Scottish Mental Survey 1932 and the Midspan Studies," *Personality and Individual Differences* 38 (2004).

11 Kelly DiNardo, "Marriage Rates Rise for Educated Women," *Women's eNews,* April 6, 2004.

12 1980 United States Census data compiled by statistician Heidi Berman.

13 John Levi Martin, "Is Power Sexy?," *American Journal of Sociology* 111, no. 2 (2005).

14 Megan M. Sweeney and Maria Cancian, "The Changing Importance of White Women's Economic Prospects for Assortative Mating," *Journal of Marriage and the Family* 66 (2004).

15 Rose, "Education and Hypergamy, and the "Success Gap."

16 Heather Boushey as cited in Garance Franke-Ruta, "Creating a Lie: Sylvia Ann Hewlett and the Myth of the Baby Bust," *American Prospect,* June 30, 2002.

17 Low education is also a risk factor for domestic violence. Sharmila Lawrence, "Domestic Violence and Welfare Policy: Research Findings That Can Inform Policies on Marriage and Child Well-Being," in *National Center for Children in Poverty* (New York: Mailman School of Public Health, Columbia University, 2002).

CHAPTER 3: HI, I'M FABULOUS

1 Christian Carter, *"Dating Advice: Why Successful Women Fail with Men"* (blast email from CatchHimandKeepHim.com, 2005 [cited October 31, 2005]).

2 Lee Rainie and Mary Madden, "Not Looking for Love: The State of Romance in America, 2006," report for the Pew Internet & American Life Project (2006), www.pewinternet.org.

3 Ibid. Thirty-eight percent of couples met at work or school, and another 34 percent met through family or friends.

4 Christian Carter, "First Impressions That Make Men Want More" (blast email from CatchHimandKeepHim.com, 2006 [cited January 27, 2006]).

5 Rachel Greenwald, *Find a Husband After 35 Using What I Learned at Harvard Business School,* 2004 edition (New York: Ballantine, 2003), pp. 22–23

6 Editor, "U.S. Dating Services Market," in *Marketdata Enterprises, Inc.* (Marketdata Enterprises, Inc., 2006).

7 Viviana Zelizer, *The Purchase of Intimacy* (Princeton, NJ: Princeton University Press, 2005), pp. 114–117.

8 Mary Madden and Amanda Lenhart, "Online Dating Activities and Pursuits," in *Pew/Internet* (Washington, DC: Pew Internet & American Life Project, 2006).

9 Richard Kirshenbaum and Daniel Rosenberg, *Closing the Deal: Two Married Guys Take You from Single Miss to Wedded Bliss* (New York: William Morrow, 2005), pp. ix and 193.

10 Greenwald, *Find a Husband After 35 Using What I Learned at Harvard Business School,* p. 83.

11 Ibid., p. 66.

12 Rachel Greenwald, *Do I Intimidate Men?* (MSN Dating & Personals, 2004 [cited February 15, 2005]).

13 Nancy Slotnick, *Turn Your Cablight On: Get Your Dream Man in 6 Months or Less* (New York: Gotham Books, 2006), p. 72.

CHAPTER 4: GENTLEMEN PREFER BRAINS

1 David M. Buss et al., "A Half Century of Mate Preferences: The Cultural Evolution of Values," *Journal of Marriage and the Family* 63 (May 2001).

2 Deborah Siegel, "The New Trophy Wife," *Psychology Today,* January/February 2004.

3 Ibid.

4 Peter M. Buston and Stephen T. Emlen, "Cognitive Process Underlying Human Mate Choice: The Relationship Between Self-Perception and Mate Preference in Western Society," *Proceedings of the National Academy of Sciences* 100, no. 15 (2003); Match.com, "New Research Shows Never-Married Single Men Want to Settle Down" (Match.com online press release: http://corp.match.com/index/newscenter_release_detail.asp?auto_index=92, 2005 [cited July 14, 2005]).

5 Carter, *Dating Advice: Why Successful Women Fail with Men.*

6 Christian Carter, "Women Men See as 'Relationship Material'" (blast email from CatchHimandKeepHim.com, 2005 [cited December 2, 2005]).

7 Heather L. Koball, "Crossing the Threshold: Men's Incomes, Attitudes Toward Provider Role, and Marriage Timing," *Sex Roles: A Journal of Research,* accessible via www.findarticles.com (2004).

8 Sue Shellenbarger, "The Latest Dating Headache: Women with High Salaries," *Wall Street Journal,* January 27, 2005.

9 Siegel, "The New Trophy Wife"; Match.com, "New Research Shows Never-Married Single Men Want to Settle Down."

Notes

CHAPTER 5: WHAT SWANS WANT

1 U.S. Census, "Years of School Completed by Persons 14 Years Old and Over, by Age, Race, and Sex: March 1971" (Washington, DC: U.S. Census Bureau, 1971).

2 Betty Friedan, *It Changed My Life* (New York: Random House, 1976), pp. 132–136; and U.S. Census data.

3 Stephanie Coontz, *The Way We Really Are: Coming to Terms with America's Changing Families* (New York: Basic Books, 1997), chapter two.

4 David M. Buss, *The Evolution of Desire: Strategies of Human Mating* (New York: Basic Books, 2003), p. 47.

5 Whitehead, "The Plight of the High-Status Woman."

6 John Tierney, "Male Pride and Female Prejudice," *New York Times,* January 3, 2006.

7 Buss et al., "A Half Century of Mate Preferences: The Cultural Evolution of Values."

8 Mervyn Cadwallader, "Marriage as a Wretched Institution," *Atlantic Monthly,* November 1966; http://www.rpi.edu/~verwyc/ohll.htm.

9 In the 1980s researchers wondered whether "those women who do have access to power by possessing monetary resources and education will value good earning capacity less." See David M. Buss and Michael Barnes, "Preferences in Human Mate Selection," *Journal of Personality and Social Psychology* 50, no. 3 (1986); and Koball, "Crossing the Threshold: Men's Incomes, Attitudes Toward Provider Role, and Marriage Timing."

10 Sweeney and Cancian, "The Changing Importance of White Women's Economic Prospects for Assortative Mating."

11 Wendy McElroy, *A Feminist Version of "Joe Millionaire"?* (ifeminists.com, 2004 [cited May 19, 2004]).

12 *Sex and the City,* episode 71, season 5.

Notes

CHAPTER 6: WHO IS MR. RIGHT?

1 Kimberly Goad, "Big-Earning Wives (and the Men Who Love Them)," *Redbook* online, 2004: http://redbook.ivillage.com/sex/0,,98605ztg-p,00.html./

2 Census, "Marital Status of the Population by Sex and Age: 2004," p. 50. With special thanks to Prof. Avner Offer at All Souls College, Oxford, for the spreadsheet that allowed the computation of these ratios.

3 Jason Fields, "America's Families and Living Arrangements: 2003," in *Current Population Reports* (Washington, DC: U.S. Census Bureau, 2004), Table 9.

4 Editor, "Marketing to the Affluent Woman."

5 Pamela Paul, "Love & Money: Get the Whole Truth," *Redbook,* November 2005. The study was conducted by Harris Interactive.

6 My advisor, Prof. Avner Offer at All Souls College, Oxford, notes that this idea originally came from Rhona Mahoney, *Kidding Ourselves: Breadwinning, Babies, and Bargaining Power* (New York: Basic Books, 1995), pp. 119 and 143.

7 Citigroup "Live Richly" advertising campaign, as seen on a New York City bus shelter and confirmed by Robert Julavits of Citigroup via email on Tuesday, May 9, 2006.

8 Tim Padgett and Frank Sikora, "Color-Blind Love," *Time,* May 12, 2003.

9 Zhenchao Qian and Daniel T. Lichter, "Crossing Racial Boundaries: Changes of Interracial Marriage in America, 1990–2000," in paper to be presented at the Population Association of America; found at http://paa2004.princeton.edu/download.asp?submissionId=40504 (Boston: 2004).

10 Steve Sailer, "Interracial Marriage Gender Gap Grows," United Press International, March 14, 2003.

11 Padgett and Sikora, "Color-Blind Love."

12 Sum et al., "Growing Gender Gaps in College Enrollment and Degree Attainment in the U.S. and Their Potential Economic and Social Consequences."

13 For more information, see: http://www.gc.cuny.edu/faculty/
research_briefs/aris/key_findings.htm.

CHAPTER 7: THE CLOCK IS ON THE FIELD?

1 Maureen Dowd, "Men Just Want Mommy," *New York Times,* January 13, 2005.

2 Census, "Marital Status of the Population by Sex and Age: 2004," table 51.

CHAPTER 8: SHATTERING THE MYTH OF THE BABY BUST

1 Goldin, "Career and Family: College Women Look to the Past," p. 51.

2 Avner Offer, *The Challenge of Affluence: Self-Control and Well-Being in the United States and Britain Since 1950* (Oxford: Oxford University Press, 2006), p. 263 (figure 11.7).

3 Rose, "Education and Hypergamy, and the 'Success Gap,'" p. 12.

4 Ibid., and personal interviews with the author.

5 Franke-Ruta, "Creating a Lie: Sylvia Ann Hewlett and the Myth of the Baby Bust."

6 Marian N. Ruderman and Patricia J. Ohlott, *Standing at the Crossroads: Next Steps for High-Achieving Women* (San Francisco: Jossey-Bass, 2002), p.3.

7 T. J. Mathews and Stephanie J. Ventura, "Birth and Fertility Rates by Educational Attainment: United States, 1994," *NCHS Monthly Vital Statistics Reports—(PHS) 97–1120* 45, no. 10 (2005).

8 Susan Saulny, "In Baby Boomlet, Preschool Derby Is the Fiercest Yet," *New York Times,* March 3, 2006.

9 T. J. Mathews and Stephanie J. Ventura, "Birth and Fertility Rates by Educational Attainment: United States, 1994." In his 2006 book, *The Challenge of Affluence,* Avner Offer notes that today, education has a much weaker influence on the number of children a woman has than it did prior to 1990. Avner Offer, *The Challenge of Affluence: Self-Control and Well-Being in the United States and Britain Since 1950,* p. 258.

10   Phone interview with Dr. Robert Howe, February 24, 2006.

11   Editor, "Assisted Reproductive Technology (ART) Report: Section 2—ART Cycles Using Fresh, Nondonor Eggs or Embryos" (Washington, DC: Department of Health and Human Services, Centers for Disease Control and Prevention, 2003).

12   Editor, "Assisted Reproductive Technology (ART) Report: Section 1—Overview" (Washington, DC: Department of Health and Human Services, Centers for Disease Control and Prevention, 2003).

13   Offer, *The Challenge of Affluence: Self-Control and Well-Being in the United States and Britain Since 1950*, p. 249.

14   Catherine Arnst, "Commentary: Women Work. The Support System Doesn't," *BusinessWeek,* November 4, 2002: http://www.businessweek.com/magazine/content/02_44/b3806046.htm.

15   Louise Story, "Many Women at Elite Colleges Set Career Path to Motherhood," *New York Times,* September 20, 2005.

16   Heather Boushey, "Are Women Opting Out? Debunking the Myth," in *CEPR Briefing Paper* (Washington, DC: Center for Economic and Policy Research, 2005).

17   Offer, *The Challenge of Affluence: Self-Control and Well-Being in the United States and Britain Since 1950*, p. 263 (figure 11.7).

18   Shauna Curphey, "Number of Stay-at-Home Dads Rising," *Women's eNews,* July 4, 2003.

19   Catalyst, "Quick Takes: Child Care" (New York: Catalyst, Inc., 2002). This report is based on U.S. Census data.

20   See http://www.cfwbr.org/topfacts.html.

CHAPTER 9: FUTURES AND OPTIONS

 1   Thornton and Young-DeMarco, "Four Decades of Trends in Attitudes Toward Family Issues in the United States: The 1960s Through the 1990s."

 2   Catalyst, "The Next Generation: Today's Professionals, Tomorrow's Leaders" (New York: Catalyst Inc., 2001).

3 Coontz, *The Way We Really Are: Coming to Terms with America's Changing Families*, p. 51.

4 Robert Schoen, Stacy Rogers, and Paul Amato, "Wives' Employment and Spouses' Marital Happiness: Assessing the Direction of Influence Using Longitudinal Couple Data," *Journal of Family Issues* 27, no. 4 (2006).

5 Coontz, *The Way We Really Are: Coming to Terms with America's Changing Families*, p. 71.

6 Jacqueline Lerner, *Working Women and Their Families* (Thousand Oaks, Calif.: Sage, 1994), pp. 45–46.

7 Hewlett, *Creating a Life: What Every Woman Needs to Know About Having a Baby and a Career*, pp. 299–300.

Bibliography

Anderson, Carol M., Susan Stewart, and Sona Dimidjian. *Flying Solo: Single Women in Midlife.* New York: W. W. Norton & Company, 1994.

Arnst, Catherine. "Commentary: Women Work. The Support System Doesn't." *BusinessWeek Online,* November 4, 2002.

Austen, Jane. *Pride and Prejudice.* In *The Novels of Jane Austen: The Text Based on Collation of the Early Editions,* edited by R. W. Chapman. Oxford: Clarendon Press, 1932.

———. "The Watsons." In *The Works of Jane Austen: Volume 6, Minor Works,* edited by R. W. Chapman. London: Oxford University Press, 1954.

Barash, Susan Shapiro. *The New Wife: The Evolving Role of the American Wife.* Lenexa, Kans.: None the Less Press, 2004.

Barker, Olivia. "Singled Out by Society's Stare." *USA Today,* February 13, 2005.

Barnett, Rosalind, and Caryl Rivers. *Same Difference: How Gender Myths Are Hurting Our Relationships, Our Children and Our Jobs.* New York: Basic Books, 2004.

Bartal, David. "Love & Marriage: Scandinavian Style." *Nordic Reach* 2005, pp. 38–45.

Bellah, Robert N., Richard Madsen, William Sullivan, Ann Swinder, and Steven Tipton. *Habits of the Heart: Individualism and Commitment in American Life,* 1996 ed. Berkeley: University of California Press, 1985.

Berman, Russell. "New Yorkers Marry Late, Report Says." *New York Sun,* October 13, 2005.

Bibliography

Bird, Laura. "Madison Avenue Stalks Today's Archetypal Male." *Wall Street Journal,* March 5, 1992, B1.

Boushey, Heather. "Are Women Opting Out? Debunking the Myth." In *CEPR Briefing Paper.* Washington, DC: Center for Economic and Policy Research, 2005.

———. " 'Baby Panic' Book Skews Data, Misses Actual Issue." *Womens eNews,* July 3, 2002.

Bressler, Eric R., and Sigal Balshine. "The Influence of Humor on Desirablity." *Evolution and Human Behavior* 27 (2006): 29–39.

Brooks, David. "Mind Over Muscle." *New York Times,* October 16, 2005, p. WK12.

———. "The Year of Domesticity." *New York Times,* January 1, 2006, p. WK8.

Brown, Helen Gurley. *Sex and the Single Girl.* 1983 ed. New York: Harper Mass Market Paperbacks, 1963.

Brown, Stephanie L., and Brian P. Lewis. "Relational Dominance and Mate Selection Criteria: Evidence That Males Attend to Female Dominance." *Evolution and Human Behavior* 25 (2004): 406–415.

Buscaglia, Leo. *Loving Each Other.* Thorofare, NJ: SLACK, 1984.

Bushnell, Candace. *Lipstick Jungle.* New York: Hyperion, 2005.

Buss, David M. *The Evolution of Desire: Strategies of Human Mating.* New York: Basic Books, 1994.

Buss, David M., and Michael Barnes. "Preferences in Human Mate Selection." *Journal of Personality and Social Psychology* 50, no. 3 (1986): 559–70.

Buss, David M., Todd K. Shackelford, Lee A. Kirkpatrick, and Randy J. Larsen. "A Half Century of Mate Preferences: The Cultural Evolution of Values." *Journal of Marriage and the Family* 63, May (2001): 491–503.

Buston, Peter M., and Stephen T. Emlen. "Cognitive Process Underlying Human Mate Choice: The Relationship Between Self-Perception and Mate Preference in Western Society." *Proceedings of the National Academy of Sciences* 100, no. 15 (July 22, 2003).

Cadwallader, Mervyn. "Marriage as a Wretched Institution." *Atlantic Monthly,* November 1966.

Bibliography

Campbell, Bebe Moor. *Successful Women, Angry Men.* 2nd revised edition. New York: Berkley Books, 2000.

Carter, Christian. *Dating Advice: Why Successful Women Fail with Men.* Blast email from CatchHimandKeepHim.com, 2005 [cited October 31, 2005].

———. *First Impressions That Make Men Want More.* Blast email from CatchHimandKeepHim.com, 2006 [cited January 27, 2006].

———. *Women Men See as "Relationship Material."* Blast email from CatchHimandKeepHim.com, 2005 [cited December 2, 2005].

Catalyst. "The Bottom Line: Connecting Corporate Performance and Gender Diversity." New York: Catalyst Inc., 2004, pp. 1–34.

———. "The Next Generation: Today's Professionals, Tomorrow's Leaders." New York: Catalyst Inc., 2001, pp. 1–72.

———. "Quick Takes: Child Care." New York: Catalyst, Inc., 2002, p. 1.

———. "Quick Takes: Women in Their 20s & 30s." New York: Catalyst Inc., 2005, p. 1.

Census, U.S. "Marital Status of the Population by Sex and Age: 2004." In *America's Families and Living Arrangements 2004,* Washington, DC: U.S. Census Bureau, 2005. http://www.census.gov/prod/2005pubs/06statab/pop.pdf.

———. "Years of School Completed by Persons 14 Years Old and Over, by Age, Race, and Sex: March 1971." Washington, DC: U.S. Census Bureau, 1971. http://www.census.gov/population/socdemo/education/p20-229/tab-01.pdf.

Census, U.S. Bureau of the. "Fertility Indicators." *National Vital Statistics Report* 48, no. 3 (2000).

Clements, Marcelle. *The Improvised Woman: Single Women Reinventing Single Life.* New York: W.W. Norton & Company, 1999.

Coontz, Stephanie. *Marriage, a History: From Obedience to Intimacy, or How Love Conquered Marriage.* New York: Viking, 2005.

———. "Three 'Rules' That Don't Apply: A Historian Upends Conventional Wisdom." *Newsweek,* June 5, 2006, p. 49.

———. *The Way We Never Were: American Families and the Nostalgia Trap.* New York: Basic Books, 1992.

————. *The Way We Really Are: Coming to Terms with America's Changing Families.* New York: Basic Books, 1997.

Curphey, Shauna. "Number of Stay-at-Home Dads Rising." *Women's eNews,* July 4, 2003.

D'Emilio, John, and Estelle B. Freedman. *Intimate Matters: A History of Sexuality in America.* New York: Harper & Row, 1988.

DiNardo, Kelly. "Marriage Rates Rise for Educated Women." *Women's eNews,* April 6, 2004.

Dobson, Roger, and Maurice Chittenden. "Clever Devils Get the Bird." *Times* (London), January 2, 2005.

Douthat, Ross. "Has Feminism Failed? Maureen Dowd Thinks So. She's Wrong." *Weekly Standard,* November 3, 2005.

Dowd, Maureen. *Are Men Necessary? When Sexes Collide.* New York: Putnam, 2005.

————. "The Baby Bust." *New York Times,* April 10, 2002.

————. "Men Just Want Mommy." *New York Times,* January 13, 2005.

————. "Powerful Male Looking for Maid to Marry." *International Herald Tribune,* January 14, 2005.

————. "What's a Modern Girl to Do?" *New York Times,* October 30, 2005.

Editor. "Alpha Females Use Their Heads, but Lose Their Hearts." *Courier-Mail,* March 1, 2005.

————. "Assisted Reproductive Technology (ART) Report: Section 1—Overview." Washington, DC: Department of Health and Human Services, Centers for Disease Control and Prevention, 2003. http://www.cdc.gov/art/art2003/section1.htm.

————. "Assisted Reproductive Technology (ART) Report: Section 2—ART Cycles Using Fresh, Nondonor Eggs or Embryos." Washington, DC: Department of Health and Human Services, Centers for Disease Control and Prevention, 2003. http://www.cdc.gov/art/art2003/sect2_fig3-13.htm#Figure%11.

————. "Divorcing Mr. Nice Guy." *More,* April 2005, pp. 99–179.

————. *High IQ Cuts Women's Marriage Prospects.* ABC Online, 2005 [cited January 3 2005].

————. "Marketing to the Affluent Woman." In *Neuberger Berman Research.* New York: Lehman Brothers Company, 2004, p. 2.

Bibliography

———. "Primary Sources: Gentlemen Prefer Brains." *Atlantic Monthly,* July/August 2004.

———. "Primary Sources: Too Smart to Marry." *Atlantic Monthly,* April 2005.

———. "They're Too Smart for These Guys." *Chicago Sun-Times,* December 15, 2004, p. 61.

———. "Too Smart to Marry?" *Atlantic Monthly,* April 1, 2005, p. 44.

———. "U.S. Dating Services Market." Tampa, Fla.: Marketdata Enterprises, Inc., 2006.

Ehrenreich, Barbara. *Bait and Switch: The (Futile) Pursuit of the American Dream.* New York: Metropolitan Books, 2005.

Ehrenreich, Barbara, and Dierdre English. *For Her Own Good: Two Centuries of the Experts' Advice to Women.* 2nd revised edition. New York: Anchor Books, 2005.

Erbe, Bonnie. "Selling Women Short—Don't Buy It." *Chicago Sun-Times,* January 5, 2005, p. 33.

Farrell, Warren. *Why Men Earn More: The Startling Truth Behind the Pay Gap—and What Women Can Do About It.* New York: The American Management Association, 2005.

Fels, Anna. "Do Women Lack Ambition?" In *On Point,* edited by Harvard Business Review, Cambridge: Harvard Business Review, 2005, pp. 29–39.

———. *Necessary Dreams: Ambition in Women's Changing Lives.* New York: Anchor Books, 2004.

Fields, Jason. "America's Families and Living Arrangements: 2003." In *Current Population Report,* U.S. Census. Washington, DC: U.S. Census Bureau, 2004.

Fisher, Helen. "This Thing Called Love: The Truth About the Urge to Merge." *Daily News,* February 9, 2005, pp. 1–3.

Fisman, Raymond, Sheena S. Iyengar, Emir Kamenica, and Itamar Simonson. "Gender Differences in Mate Selection: Evidence from a Speed Dating Experiment." *Quarterly Journal of Economics,* to be published 2006.

Franke-Ruta, Garance. "Creating a Lie: Sylvia Ann Hewlett and the Myth of the Baby Bust." *American Prospect,* June 30, 2002.

Bibliography

Friedan, Betty. *It Changed My Life.* New York: Random House, 1976.

Geller, Jaclyn. *Here Comes the Bride: Women, Weddings and the Marriage Mystique.* New York: Four Walls Eight Windows, 2001.

Gibson, Valerie. "Dateless Women Need to Soften Up." *Calgary Sun,* January 28, 2004.

Giddens, Anthony. *The Transformation of Intimacy: Sexuality, Love & Eroticism in Modern Societies.* Stanford, Calif.: Stanford University Press, 1992.

Gladwell, Malcolm. *The Tipping Point: How Little Things Can Make a Big Difference.* Boston: Little, Brown & Co., 2000.

Glenn, Norval, and Elizabeth Marquardt. "Hooking Up, Hanging Out, and Hoping for Mr. Right: College Women on Dating and Mating Today." Washington, DC: Independent Women's Forum, 2001.

Goad, Kimberly. "Big-Earning Wives (and the Men Who Love Them)." *Redbook* 2004, published at http://magazines.ivillage.com/redbook/sex/happy/articles/0,,284445_669656,00.html.

Goldin, Claudia. "Career and Family: College Women Look to the Past." In *Gender and Family Issues in the Workplace,* edited by Francine D. Blau and Ronald G. Ehrenberg. New York: Russell Sage Foundation, 1997.

———. "Making a Name: Women's Surnames at Marriage and Beyond." *Journal of Economic Perspectives* 18, no. 2 (2004): 143–160.

———. "Working It Out." *New York Times,* March 15, 2006, p. A27.

Goldin, Claudia, and Lawrence F. Katz. "Career and Marriage in the Age of the Pill." *American Economic Review, Papers and Proceedings,* 2005.

Goldin, Claudia, and Maria Shim. "Making a Name: Women's Surnames at Marriage and Beyond." *Journal of Economic Perspectives* 18, no. 2 (2004): 143–160.

Gottlieb, Lori. "How Do I Love Thee?" *Atlantic Monthly,* March 2006, pp. 58–70.

———. "The Xy Files." *Atlantic Monthly,* September 2005, pp. 141–150.

Gravitch, Diana. "Love and Money Survey." Edited by Harris Interactive. 2005.

Bibliography

Gray, John. *Men Are from Mars, Women Are from Venus.* New York: HarperCollins, 1992.

Greenwald, Rachel. *Do I Intimidate Men?* MSN Dating & Personals, 2004 [cited February 15, 2005].

———. *Find a Husband After 35 Using What I Learned at Harvard Business School.* New York: Ballantine, 2003.

Hakim, Catherine. *Key Issues in Women's Work: Female Heterogeneity and the Polarization of Women's Employment.* London: Athlone, 1996.

Harmanci, Reyhan. "Women's Pages: Next Time You Read About 'What Women Want,' Check the Research—It's Likely to Be Flimsy." *San Francisco Chronicle,* January 4, 2006, p. E1.

Hayden, Naura. *How to Satisfy a Woman* Every Time . . . *And Have Her Beg for More.* 2001 ed. New York: Bibli O'Phile, 1982.

Hecht, Randy B. *Gentlemen Prefer . . . Brains?* MSN Dating & Personals, 2006 [cited June 7, 2006].

Hewlett, Sylvia Ann. *Creating a Life: What Every Woman Needs to Know About Having a Baby and a Career.* New York: Hyperion, 2002.

———. "Executive Women and the Myth of Having It All." In *On Point,* edited by Harvard Business Review. Cambridge: Harvard Business Review, 2005, pp. 1–12.

Hewlett, Sylvia Ann, and Carolyn Buck Luce. "Off-Ramps and On-Ramps: Keeping Talented Women on the Road to Success." In *On Point,* edited by Harvard Business Review. Cambridge: Harvard Business Review, 2005, pp. 16–27.

Hewlett, Sylvia Ann, and Norma Vite-Leon. "High-Achieving Women, 2001." New York: The National Parenting Association, 2002, pp. 1–60.

Hochschild, Arlie. "The Commercial Spirit of Intimate Life and the Abduction of Feminism: Signs from Women's Advice Books." *Theory, Culture and Society* 11 (1994): 1–24.

———. *The Commercialization of Intimate Life: Notes from Home and Work.* Berkeley: University of California Press, 2003.

———. *The Managed Heart: Commercialization of Human Feeling.* Berkeley: University of California Press, 1983.

———. *The Second Shift.* London: Piatkus, 1990.

Hoffmann, Bill. "First and Lust: N.Y. Men Go for Sex in Free Time—but Gals Want Family and Friends." *New York Post,* March 3, 2005, p. 25.

Holland, Dorothy C., and Margaret A. Eisenhart. *Educated in Romance: Women, Achievement, and College Culture.* 1992 paperback ed. Chicago: University of Chicago Press, 1990.

Hourihane, Ann Marie. "Keep Young and Stupidful If You Want to Be Loved." *Sunday Tribune* (Dublin), January 30, 2005, p. 3.

Hurley, Dan. "Divorce Rate: It's Not as High as You Think." *New York Times,* April 19, 2005, F7.

Israel, Betsy. *Bachelor Girl: 100 Years of Breaking the Rules—a Social History of Living Single.* New York: Perennial, 2003.

Johnson, M. P. "Commitment to Personal Relationships." In *Advances in Personal Relationships: A Research Manual,* edited by W. H. Jones and D. Perlman. London: J. Kingsley, 1991, pp. 117–143.

Kasser, Tim. *The High Price of Materialism.* Cambridge: MIT Press, 2002.

Kelly, Kristin. "New Research Shows Never-Married Single Men Want to Settle Down." Press Release from Match.com and *Marie Claire* survey, 2005.

Kent, Melissa. "Here Dumbs the Bride." *West Australian* (Perth), January 15, 2005, p. 3.

Kingston, Anne. *The Meaning of Wife: A Provocative Look at Women and Marriage in the Twenty-First Century.* Paperback ed. New York: Picador, 2004.

———. "Why Women Can't Get Ahead." *Report on Business,* December 2005, pp. 57–71.

Kirshenbaum, Richard, and Daniel Rosenberg. *Closing the Deal: Two Married Guys Take You from Single Miss to Wedded Bliss.* New York: William Morrow, 2005.

Koball, Heather L. "Crossing the Threshold: Men's Incomes, Attitudes Toward Provider Role, and Marriage Timing." *Sex Roles: A Journal of Research,* accessible via www.findarticles.com (2004).

Kurtz, Howard. "Sex and the Single Stiletto." *Washington Post,* November 5, 2005, p. C1.

Bibliography

Kurtz, Stanley. "Don't Take Your Daughter to Work." *National Review,* April 11, 2002.

Labi, Nadya. "The Baby Gamble." *Yale Alumni Magazine,* March/April 2006, pp. 36–43.

Landsburg, Steven E. "The Price of Motherhood: Ready to Have a Baby? You'll Earn 10 Percent More If You Wait a Year." *Slate,* December 9, 2005.

Lawrence, Sharmila. "Domestic Violence and Welfare Policy: Research Findings That Can Inform Policies on Marriage and Child Well-Being." In *National Center for Children in Poverty.* New York: Mailman School of Public Health, Columbia University, 2002.

Lawson, Willow. "Humor's Sexual Side." *Psychology Today,* September/October 2005.

Lee, Gary R. "Marriage and Anomie: A Causal Argument." *Journal of Marriage and the Family* 36, no. 3 (1974): 523–532.

Lerner, Jacqueline. *Working Women and Their Families.* Thousand Oaks, Calif.: Sage, 1994.

Lewin, Tamar. "Data on Marriage and Births Reflect the Political Divide." *New York Times,* October 13, 2005.

———. "A Marriage of Unequals: When Richer Weds Poorer, Money Isn't the Only Difference." *New York Times,* May 19, 2005, pp. A1–A14.

Lewis, Jane. *The End of Marriage? Individualism and Intimate Relations.* Cheltenham, UK: Edward Elgar, 2001.

———. "Individualism and Commitment in Marriage and Cohabitation." *Lord Chancellor's Research Programme Series* 99, no. 8 (1999).

Lewis, Karen Gail. *With or Without a Man: Single Women Taking Control of Their Lives.* Annapolis, Md.: Bull Publishing, 2001.

Lublin, Joann S. "A Career Wife Complicates the CEO's Life." *Wall Street Journal,* December 15, 1994, p. B1.

Lundberg, Shelly, and Elaina Rose. "The Determinants of Specialization within Marriage." Preliminary working paper from the economics department at the University of Washington, 1999, pp. 1–35.

Macko, Lia, and Kerry Rubin. *Midlife Crisis at 30: How the Stakes Have Changed for a New Generation—and What to Do About It.* New York: Rodale, 2004.

Madden, Mary, and Amanda Lenhart. "Online Dating Activities and Pursuits." Report for the Pew Internet and American Life Project, 2006. www.pewinternet.org.

Mahoney, Rhona. *Kidding Ourselves: Breadwinning, Babies, and Bargaining Power.* New York: Basic Books, 1995.

Martin, John Levi. "Is Power Sexy?" *American Journal of Sociology* 111, no. 2 (2005): 408–446.

Mathews, T. J., and Stephanie J. Ventura. "Birth and Fertility Rates by Educational Attainment: United States, 1994." *NCHS Monthly Vital Statistics Reports—(PHS) 97-1120* 45, no. 10 (2005): 20.

May, Amanda. "Successful Women: Undateable?" Match.com, May 14, 2006, online at http://www.match.com/magazine/article0.aspx?articleid=5886.

McElroy, Wendy. *A Feminist Version of "Joe Millionaire"?* ifeminists.com, 2004 [cited May 19, 2004].

McGinn, Daniel. "Marriage by the Numbers: Twenty Years Since the Infamous 'Terrorist' Line, States of Unions Aren't What We Predicted They'd Be." *Newsweek,* June 5, 2006, pp. 40–48.

McLaughlin, Steven D., Barbara Melber, John Billy, Denise Zimmerle, Linda Winges, and Terry Johnson. *The Changing Lives of American Women.* Chapel Hill: University of North Carolina Press, 1988.

Minetor, Randi. *Breadwinner Wives and the Men They Marry: How to Have a Successful Marriage While Outearning Your Husband.* Far Hills, NJ: New Horizon Press, 2000.

Morgan, Marabel. *The Total Woman.* Old Tappan, NJ: Fleming H. Revell Company, 1973.

Morris, Betsy. "How Corporate America Is Betraying Women." *Fortune,* January 10, 2005, pp. 64–70.

Offer, Avner. "Body Weight and Self-Control in the United States and Britain Since the 1950s." *Social History of Medicine* 14, no. 1 (2001): 79–106.

Bibliography

——. *The Challenge of Affluence: Self-Control and Well-Being in the United States and Britain Since 1950.* Oxford: Oxford University Press, 2006.

——. "From Regard to Reward: Mating and Unmating in the United States and Britain Since 1945." In an unpublished discussion paper, 1999.

Oldenburg, Don. "The Sexes: KO'ing American Husbands." *Washington Post,* November 3, 1988, p. C05.

Padgett, Tim, and Frank Sikora. "Color-Blind Love." *Time,* May 12, 2003, p. A8.

Paul, Pamela. "Love & Money: Get the Whole Truth." *Redbook,* November 2005.

Pearce, Tralee. "Want to Move Up? Marry Down." *Globe and Mail,* May 13, 2006.

Pearson, Allison. *I Don't Know How She Does It.* Paperback ed. New York: Anchor Books, 2002.

Peskowitz, Miriam. *The Truth Behind the Mommy Wars: Who Decides What Makes a Good Mother?* Emeryville, Calif.: Seal Press, 2005.

Pine, Joseph, and James H. Gilmore. "Welcome to the Experience Economy." *Harvard Business Review,* July-August 1998: 97–105.

Pocius, Marilyn. "Women Who Read Too Much: The 10-Minute Intervention for Self-Help Addiction." *Chicago Tribune,* July 11, 2001, p. 1.

Pollitt, Katha. "Backlash Babies." *The Nation,* May 13, 2002.

Qian, Zhenchao, and Daniel T. Lichter. "Crossing Racial Boundaries: Changes of Interracial Marriage in America, 1990–2000." Paper presented at the Population Association of America, found at http://paa2004.princeton.edu/download.asp?submissionId=40504, 2004.

Rainie, Lee, and Mary Madden. "Not Looking for Love: The State of Romance in America, 2006." Report for the Pew Internet & American Life Project, 2006. www.pewinternet.org.

Ravicz, Simone. *High on Stress: A Woman's Guide to Optimizing the Stress in Her Life.* Oakland, Calif.: New Harbinger Publications, Inc., 1998.

Ray, L. "The American Woman in the Mass Media." In *Toward a Sociology of Women,* edited by Constantina Safilios-Rothschild, Lexington, Mass.: Xerox College Publishing, 1972.

Rivers, Caryl, and Rosalind Chait Barnett. "Men Prefer Sexy, Smart Unstepfords, Yes, Really." *Women's eNews,* August 4, 2004.

———. "Why Maureen Dowd Doesn't Know What Men Really Want." *Women's eNews,* November 2, 2005.

Robbins, Alexandra, and Abby Wilner. *Quarterlife Crisis.* New York: Tarcher/Putnam, 2001.

Roberts, Sam. "So Many Men, So Few Women." *New York Times,* February 12, 2006, WK3.

Roiphe, Katie. "Is Maureen Dowd Necessary?" *Slate,* November 2, 2005.

Rose, Elaina. "Does Education Really Disadvantage Women in the Marriage Market?" Working paper no. 33, Center for Statistics and the Social Sciences at the University of Washington, 2003.

———. "Education and Hypergamy, and the 'Success Gap.'" Working paper no. 53 (updated version of working paper no. 33, "Does Education Really Disadvantage Women in the Marriage Market?"), Center for Statistics and the Social Sciences at the University of Washington, 2005.

———. "A Joint Econometric Model of Marriage and Partner Choice." Working paper no. 58, Center for Statistics and the Social Sciences at the University of Washington, originally released in 2004, updated in 2006.

———. "Marriage and Assortative Mating: How Have the Patterns Changed?" Working paper no. 22, Center for Statistics and the Social Sciences at the University of Washington, originally released in 2001, updated in 2002.

Rose, Marla Matzer. "Women Achievers Profiled." *Cincinnati Enquirer,* December 7, 2005, p. 7D.

Ruderman, Marian N., and Patricia J. Ohlott. *Standing at the Crossroads: Next Steps for High-Achieving Women.* San Francisco: Jossey-Bass, 2002.

Ryan, John. "Martial Status, Happiness and Anomia." *Journal of Marriage and the Family* 43, no. 3 (1981): 643–649.

Bibliography

Sacks, Glenn. "Dowd on Women and the 'Baby Bust': It's All Men's Fault." www.liberator.net, 2002 [cited April 21, 2002].

Safier, Rachel. "Living Single." *Salon,* December 14, 2005.

Sailer, Steve. "Interracial Marriage Gender Gap Grows." United Press International, March 14, 2003.

Saulny, Susan. "In Baby Boomlet, Preschool Derby Is the Fiercest Yet." *New York Times,* March 3, 2006, p. 1.

Schlessinger, Laura. *Ten Stupid Things Men Do to Mess Up Their Lives.* New York: HarperCollins, 1997.

Schoen, Robert, Stacey Rogers, and Paul Amato. "Wives' Employment and Spouses Marital Happiness: Assessing the Direct Influence Using Longitudinal Couple Data." *Journal of Family Issues* 27, no. 4 (2006): 506–528.

Schwartz, John. "Glass Ceilings at Altar as Well as Boardroom." *New York Times,* December 14, 2004, p. 7.

Shafer, Jack. "A Trend So New It's Old." *Slate,* September 23, 2005.

Shalizi, Cosma Rohilla. "Mate Choice, or, You Don't Always Know What You Want." In *Three-Toed Sloth* blog, July 12, 2003.

Shellenbarger, Sue. "The Latest Dating Headache: Women with High Salaries." *Wall Street Journal,* January 27, 2005, p. D1.

Siegel, Deborah. "The New Trophy Wife." *Psychology Today,* January/February 2004, p. 52.

Simcik, Elsa K. "Sexy, Successful . . . And Single?" MSN Dating & Personals, 2006. Online at: http://msn.match.com/msn/article.aspx?articleid=5001&menuid=6&lid=0.

Slotnick, Nancy. *Turn Your Cablight On: Get Your Dream Man in 6 Months or Less.* New York: Gotham Books, 2006.

Sohn, Amy. "No Sex, No Baby." *New York,* June 6, 2005, p. 56.

South, Scott J. "Sociodemographic Differentials in Mate Selection Preferences." *Journal of Marriage and the Family* 53, no. 4 (1991): 928–940.

Steiner, Leslie Morgan, ed. *Mommy Wars: Stay-at-Home and Career Moms Face Off on Their Choices, Their Lives, Their Families.* New York: Random House, 2006.

Story, Louise. "Many Women at Elite Colleges Set Career Path to Motherhood." *New York Times,* September 20, 2005, A1.

Straus, Jillian. *Unhooked Generation: The Truth About Why We're Still Single.* New York: Hyperion, 2006.

Sum, Andrew, Neeta Fogg, Paul Harrington, Ishwar Khatiwada, Sheila Palma, Nathan Pond, and Paulo Tobar. "Growing Gender Gaps in College Enrollment and Degree Attainment in the U.S. and Their Potential Economic and Social Consequences." Washington, DC: Prepared for the Business Roundtable by the Center for Labor Market Studies at Northeastern University, 2003.

Sweeney, Megan M., and Maria Cancian. "The Changing Importance of White Women's Economic Prospects for Assortative Mating." *Journal of Marriage and the Family* 66 (2004): 1015–1028.

Tanenbaum, Leora. *Catfight: Rivalries Among Women—from Diets to Dating, from the Boardroom to the Delivery Room.* 2003 paperback ed. New York: Perennial, 2002.

Taylor, Michelle D., Carole L. Hart, George Davey Smith, Lawrence J. Whalley, David J. Hole, Valerie Wilson, and Ian J. Deary. "Childhood IQ and Marriage by Mid-Life: The Scottish Mental Survey 1932 and the Midspan Studies." *Personality and Individual Differences* 38 (2004): 1621–1630.

Thornton, Arland, and Linda Young-DeMarco. "Four Decades of Trends in Attitudes Toward Family Issues in the United States: The 1960s Through the 1990s." *Journal of Marriage and the Family* 63 (November 2001): 1009–1037.

Tichenor, Veronica Jaris. *Earning More and Getting Less: Why Successful Wives Can't Buy Equality.* New Brunswick, NJ: Rutgers University Press, 2005.

Tierney, John. "Male Pride and Female Prejudice." *New York Times,* January 3, 2006, p. A17.

———. "What Women Want." *New York Times,* May 24, 2005.

Toufexis, Anastasia. "When the Ring Doesn't Fit." *Psychology Today,* December 1996.

Trimberger, E. Kay. *The New Single Woman.* Boston: Beacon Press, 2005.

Bibliography

UPI Newswires. "Men Prefer to Wed Secretary." UPI Newswires, December 13, 2004.

Van Buren, Abigail. "Smart Single Women Despair of Ever Finding True Love." uexpress.com, December 21, 2005.

———. "Smart Single Women Despair of Ever Finding True Love (Dear Abby)." www.uexpress.com, December 22, 2005.

Vanzant, Iyanla. *In the Meantime: Finding Yourself and the Love That You Want.* 1999 ed. London: Simon & Schuster, 1997.

Veroff, Joseph, Elizabeth Douvan, and Richard Kulka. *The Inner American: A Self-Portrait from 1957–1976.* New York: Basic Books, 1981.

Walsh, Joan. "The Baby Panic." Salon.com, April 23, 2002.

Warner, Judith. *Perfect Madness: Motherhood in the Age of Anxiety.* New York: Riverhead Books, 2005.

Wee, Louisa. *"Do Men Want Successful Women?"* virtualreporter.org, 2003 [cited May 5 2003].

Wellington, Sheila. *Be Your Own Mentor: Strategies from Top Women on the Secrets of Success.* New York: Random House, 2001.

Whelan, Elizabeth M. *A Baby . . . Maybe? A Guide to Making the Most Fateful Decision of Your Life.* New York: Bobbs-Merrill, 1975.

———. "Confessions of a Superwoman." *Across the Board,* December 1980, pp. 17–25.

Whitehead, Barbara Dafoe. "The Plight of the High-Status Woman." *Atlantic Monthly,* December 1999, pp. 120–124.

———. *Why There Are No Good Men Left: The Romantic Plight of the New Single Woman.* New York: Broadway Books, 2003.

Young, Cathy. "The Postfeminism Mommy Track." *Boston Globe,* September 26, 2005, Op-Ed Page.

Zelizer, Viviana. *The Purchase of Intimacy.* Princeton, NJ: Princeton University Press, 2005.

Zimmerman, Toni Schindler, Kristen E. Holm, and Shelley A. Haddock. "A Decade of Advice for Women and Men in the Best-Selling Self-Help Literature." *Family Relations* 50 (2001): 122–133.

Acknowledgments

It's just my name on the cover of this book, but it took the support, expertise, and kindness of hundreds of people to make this project happen.

My parents, Elizabeth and Stephen Whelan, are my mentors and cheering squad all rolled into one. From brainstorming sessions to detailed readings of every draft and contract, they supported me each step of the way. Thank you, thank you, thank you.

Deepest thanks to my agent, Emma Parry, who believed in me long before I ever came up with a salable idea, and expertly guided me through my first book. Along with the help of her assistant, Kate Scherler, I was in the best of hands from the start.

I owe gratitude and huge thanks to the entire Simon & Schuster team, and most of all to my truly gifted editor, Denise Roy, who was always available for advice and counsel. Thanks also to her assistant, Annie Orr.

The stories in this book are all true. They are the lives and experiences of more than a hundred men and women nationwide. Each of these interviewees took hours out of his or her busy life to share very personal thoughts with me. You know who you are. Thank you for making this book possible. And thank you to the dozens of friends who reached out to link me up with so many well-spoken and generous subjects.

Acknowledgments

Thanks to all my friends, advisors, and colleagues who heard me out as my arguments were still forming—and kept listening for many more months—especially Andrew Brown, Martin Callinan, Mike Cullen, Don Drakeman, Garance Franke-Ruta, Anna Fels, Gail Hodges, Carter Ingram, Jody Johannessen, Catherine Jenkins, David Kahn, Christopher Mackie, Avner Offer, Sarah Percy, Alexcis Reynolds, John Riina, Brian Rokus, Jessica Shattuck Flugge, Chelsea Vaughn, and Laura Vaughn.

A writer needs a writer's community. My heartfelt thanks to Nic Kelman, Susan Nagel, Naomi Riley, Margie Rosen, Courtney Sheinmel, and Nanar Yoseloff for keeping me focused (and typing).

The arguments in this book are underpinned with data from dozens of sources. Many, many thanks to Heidi Berman, my statistician throughout the bulk of the research, and advisory statisticians Henry Maldonado and Emilia Simeonova, for help deciphering and cross-checking Current Population Survey data. Michele Salomon and Tammy Doolittle were integral to the conception, collection, and output of the original Harris Interactive data in this book.

John Asker at New York University, Katherine Ho and Raymond Fisman at Columbia University, Claudia Goldin at Harvard University, Elaina Rose at the University of Washington, Robert Howe at the Reproductive Science Center of New England, and John O'Grady at Mercy Medical Center in Boston also gave generously of their time and academic expertise.

Christian Carter, Eric Columbus, Ken Deckinger, Randi Minetor, and Nancy Slotnick are just some of the many experts who kindly granted me interviews for this research. Heather Boushey at the Center for Economic and Policy Research; Viviana Zelizer at Princeton University; Susan Shapiro Barash and Jennifer Beaugrand; and Robert Howe were kind enough to read and offer comments on advance copies of the manuscript.

Thanks to David Smith, librarian to the stars, at the New York

Acknowledgments

Public Library for his unfailing assistance with yet another Whelan research project; to Renee DiNicola for her transcription skills; and to Alan Kaufman for his legal advice. Special thanks to my photographer Andrew Brucker, the St. John department at Saks Fifth Avenue for the clothing for the photo shoot, and Zohar Wolf at Bobbi Brown for working wonders with makeup.

And last but certainly not least, a lifetime of love and thanks to my fiancé Peter Moyers, for not running away on that first date when I told him what this book was going to be about—and for constantly making me smile along the way.